The M Who Lost his Face

دكتور عبداللطيف
شكري الله على كتابتل معوف الكتاب
أحس انـ ادركك والد لم أقابلك
مع تحياتي

عبدالرحمن

By

Abdelrahman Abdalaziz

MAPLE
PUBLISHERS

The Man Who Lost His Face

Author: Abdelrahman Abdalaziz

Copyright © 2025 Abdelrahman Abdalaziz

The author asserts the moral right to be identified as the author of this work.

The right of Abdelrahman Abdalaziz to be identified as author of this work has been asserted by the author in accordance with section 77 and 78 of the Copyright, Designs and Patents Act 1988.

First Published in 2025

ISBN 978-1-83538-768-9 (Paperback)
       978-1-83538-769-6 (Hardback)
       978-1-83538-770-2 (E-Book)

Cover Design and Book Layout by:
       Maple Publishers
       www.maplepublishers.com

Published by:
       Maple Publishers
       Fairbourne Drive, Atterbury,
       Milton Keynes,
       MK10 9RG, UK
       www.maplepublishers.com

Dedication

To all WHO staff who risk their lives, in conflict zones, to save the lives of others.

Contents

Acknowledgement

When I met Dr Omer Mekki at his flat in Paddington, London, in late January 2023, I didn't have the foggiest idea that the meeting will mark the first step in a journey eventually leading to a publishable literary work. After three hours of recording and four cups of tea, I was amazed by the remarkable memory of Dr Omer considering what he had gone through. I am indebted to him for allowing me to write his story and for his patience answering my many questions, sometimes over the phone at ungodly hours. My thanks to Dr Omer's wife, Thuraya, for filling in some of the gaps. My sincere thanks to my colleague Dr Nawal Kurdofani, and Professor Hassan Mekki for going over the manuscript and for their invaluable comments and suggestions. Special thanks to Professor, Sir David Nabarro, and Dr Abdullateef Saeed for writing the forward and the introduction respectively. Thanks to Dr Ahmed Alkurdofani for supplying the map of Sudan. I am extremely grateful to my family for their support and encouragement.

Why I wrote this book

Dr Omer and I were classmates for five years in the University of Khartoum Medical School. After graduation we lost contact for more than twenty-five years. I came to know about him being severely injured in an explosion in Baghdad a couple of years after the incident. Then I met him in one of our annual group gatherings in Khartoum where he told me about the incident and its aftermath. I was intrigued by the story, so I looked into what was written about the incident. This included details of the incident itself in newspapers and TV channels websites, and interviews with survivors and relatives of the deceased and some UN and WHO officials. There was no mention of Dr Omer and that's one reason for writing the book. The other reason is to highlight the fact, and to remind people, that humanitarian workers who provide for the needy are being targeted and killed. That doesn't make any sense. This is more relevant nowadays if we see what is happening in the conflict in the middle east where Israel has deliberately targeted and killed hundreds of aid workers. If this is allowed to go unpunished then I am afraid that humanitarian organizations will soon run out of recruits and volunteers to go and help in conflict zones. The third reason is to show Dr Omer as an example of unselfishness, perseverance and dedication and bigheartedness which is common to all those who work in the humanitarian organizations. I salute them all and hope that some sort of formula is reached to give them protection and facilitate their humanitarian mission.

⟡

Introduction

*T*his book seems like two different books. One about Osman and the other about Osmans son Dr Omer. The first part is fictional but could be regarded as a generic story applicable to many others, while the second part is factual.

Osman is a young man from a village called Artimoga in Northern Sudan. He received only primary education but aspired for a better life away from his little village and went to Khartoum to get it. He was a simple villager who dreaded needles and believed that if he married a town girl he would have a child half human and half alien. To become a policeman was all what he expects to get as a job in Khartoum. Suddenly sheer luck turned to his side when he was employed in a big trade store in Khartoum. Through hard work and dedication, he impressed his rich employer who promoted him to a manager. Later he was transferred to Hasahisa where he bought a big house on the banks of the Blue Nile, owned a car, and opened a bank account. He married a beautiful girl from Hasahisa and by doing so, he abandoned his niece whom he was expected to marry, not caring about the social boycott to his family by the other villagers in Artimoga.

Had his first baby, Omer, later to be Dr Omer. Here the first part of the book ended. Though this part is a fully fledged melodrama, but its language is good, correct, and inspiring and at times romantic.

The second part of the book started with Omer indulging into a successful line of education which led him finally to the Faculty of Medicine, University of Khartoum and hence became a doctor. He developed deep liking for Public Health as he believes that prevention is better and cheaper than cure. Through that line he achieved preeminent fame as an excellent Polio and other childhood diseases eradicator. Had it not been for the Muslim governmental authority, which Dr Omer opposed, he could have continued to work in Sudan and serve his people, but he was forced to go to Saudi Arabia followed by his good reputation as a Polio basher. Because of this reputation he was head-hunted by the WHO to work in Iraq. Unfortunately, he found himself in the gravely tragic Canal Hotel explosion. Iraq was then under American occupation.

Dr Omer suffered horrific, and devastating wounds to his face, head, and neck. What happened to him was a unique story of human suffering that should be published, read and recognised. He was taken time and time again to the operating room for craniotomy operations to remove blood clots from around his brain and to be subjected to multiple skin grafts, and reconstructive procedures to cover defects in his cheek and neck. Also, half of his skull and facial bones is replaced by Titanium (the Titanium man). These operations continued for six months, a suffering beyond normal human bearing.

When the blast occurred, Dr Omer was mistakenly mixed with injured American personnel and was flown to Balad in Iraq, then to Kuwait, and then to Germany and he was labelled as John Doe (an un-identified American soldier). Later on, he was rightly identified as a Sudanese working for the WHO and was flown to Geneva, Switzerland. There, his wife Thurayia joined him. Allas, she stepped on a wet patch and broke her leg; as if to be united with her husband in misery and suffering after previous emotional unification.

Dr Omer overtook all that unspeakable tragedy and recovered gradually to be re-employed in Iraq(again), Jordan, Pakistan and Somalia. His doctors wondered how he retained a good memory and didn't suffer any physical or psychological handicap. Notwithstanding all that, Dr Omer kept his sense of humour: when his wallet was brought to him together with his shredded trousers, he exclaimed: "If these are my trousers, how come that my legs are safe"! He joked about the precious metal that was used to build his face and considered it as a (future fortune).

Would we be exaggerating if we call Dr Omer a hero? If I am to rename this book, I shall call it: The man who lost and regained his face.

Dr Omer is grateful to all those who helped him and saved his life after the blast as he was in deep coma for five days. He is also very thankful to the numerous friends who helped while he was in hospital. Thankful to all the medical staff who treated him. Thanks to the Americans despite the fact that they were not meaning him by their care but meant to help their own John Doe. Special thanks to the WHO and its honourable employees.

Dr Abdullateef Saeed, PhD.

Teacher of literature and translation, at Sudanese Universities.

Forword

*T*his is a readable and most inspiring story about the origins and life of Dr Omer Mekki, a highly effective and well-regarded Public Health Physician from Sudan, who served with the World Health Organization in Iraq. It describes the context of the tragic event that changed the lives of Dr Omer Mekki and his family, and many other people, in Baghdad on August 19th, 2003. It is a wonderful account of his bravery and commitment, and of the ways in which different groups wove together when supporting his extraordinary recovery. It really is a story of hope and shows humanity at its best.

Here is the background. I had met Dr Omer Mekki in mid-August, in Baghdad. At the time I was responsible for the Health Action in Crisis Department at WHO headquarters in Geneva. I had joined Dr Mohamed Jama, who was the Deputy Regional Director from WHO's Eastern Mediterranean Office in Cairo, Dr Jean Jacques Frere from the World Bank, and around 20 Iraqi and international colleagues, at a meeting convened by the provisional authority governing Iraq (the CPA). Our focus was on options for quickly reconnecting different elements of Iraqi health services and enabling them to function - throughout the country.

Dr Omer Mekki, who had been working for some years in WHO's Iraq office, was part of this consultation. He provided valuable insights given his familiarity with the health challenges being faced by Iraqi people and the ways in which health services had been functioning.

On August 19th, after our consultation had ended, a group of us had crossed Baghdad to the UN headquarters in the Canal Hotel. Our task was to present the results of our work to Sergio di Mello, the highly experienced Brazilian diplomat, UN Special Representative, and leader of the UN operation in Iraq, and other colleagues. One of these was

Nadia Yunus, the highly effective WHO Executive Director in charge of External Relations and Governing Bodies who had been seconded to Sergio's team to work as his chief of staff. Our meeting was due to take place at 4.30 pm. Just as we were moving to Sergio's office, there was a huge explosion as a bomb went off.

In the immediate aftermath, as we started to see the extent of damage and human suffering, it was we UN system personnel who established a reception area in the yard outside the hotel. Security officers went systematically through what was left of the building to find survivors and casualties. They evacuated those who could walk and aided those who were injured to be extricated safely. They set up a triage facility to select, provide first aid to, and mark those who needed urgent evacuation.

US military helicopters started to arrive after about twenty minutes and took over from us. They were extraordinarily helpful and proficient, quickly bringing in extra capacity once they realized that this was an extremely serious incident. It soon became clear that Sergio Viero di Mello, was trapped in the building after the explosion. He was still alive but critically ill. He died before he could be rescued. Our colleague Nadia Yunus was killed in the explosion: the WHO tribute mourned the loss of "one of its most respected, effective and charismatic officials". Twenty-one other UN and other humanitarian workers lost their lives at the time and many more had life-changing injuries, some of which shortened their lives.

Mercifully, I emerged with just cuts and bruises. However, it could have been so much worse. That moment changed my life: it constantly reminds me that the use of violence within a conflict has immense, long term, human costs for so many people who have absolutely no stake in that conflict. Each time non-combatants are attacked, mistreated, injured and traumatised, their families and friends' lives change too, often irreversibly. They navigate pain and grief as they rebuild their lives, drawing on as many of their reserves and attributes as they can muster, but life is never the same.

Dr Omer Mekki's story reminds us that prompt medical and psychological interventions, as well as close family support, can do so much to help in aiding recovery and reducing pain and grief. He is able to continue his service thanks to the generosity and skills of those who intervened – not just immediately after the explosion, but through the dark and difficult days afterwards.

The many organizations and individuals that selflessly helped him along his journey are all to be credited for their consistent compassion and effective collaboration. They reflect the best of humanity. I would like to single out the US, WHO, UN, Swiss, Iraqi and many other health care workers, and their teams, who have helped him and his family immediately after the explosion and during his arduous recovery. I met him recently and have seen how he has benefited enormously from consistent and caring support from his extraordinary family and many friends. I also appreciate the significance of the professional and financial backing that has been provided by different parts of the World Health Organization and the UN system.

Most of all, this book helps readers to appreciate who Dr Omer Mekki is as a person. It explains how, after he recovered following numerous operations in multiple hospitals, he returned to work in Iraq and other countries in the region. He wanted to continue serving people whose lives are damaged when societies resort to violence during conflicts. His humility and bravery are widely appreciated and equip him to be an effective and valued stimulus for tackling conflicts without violence. His approach is based on open dialogue rather than intimidation or coercion, and I have seen how it works. It is one that I seek to emulate.

Professor Sir David Nabarro,

Strategic Director 4SD Foundation, Geneva

Co-Director, Institute of Global Health Innovation,

Imperial College London

Chapter 1

THE VILLAGE

*A*rtimoga. *What a nice name and a fitting one too. It literally means the fertile land or the fertile island. Artimoga is a small village sitting lazily on the banks of Nile, in northern Sudan. It lives a healthy life, sleeping early, waking up early, drinks blessed water directly from the Nile, breathes fresh air and has no idea what air pollution means, the land provides fresh organic produce which goes directly to the cooking pot and the animals are more than happy to offer milk, eggs, and meat, as if they are honouring a contract struck between them and the village people.*

Nothing much changes here. Every morning the sun rises from the east, creeping up stealthily from behind the opposite riverbank, and every evening sets in the west behind those grey mountains. The Nile continues to flow in the South Westerly direction, following the obtuse bend in its course, before turning northwards on its long journey to Egypt. It has been doing this for millions of years without going on holiday or having a weekend off. Sometimes it gets angry in the rainy season. Without giving a reason, it floods and submerges land beyond its banks, destroying villages in the process. As a kind of apology, it adds more fertility to the soil after retreating to its known boundary. Its apology is usually accepted by villagers who start expecting bumper harvests for years to come. Artimoga was on the receiving end of many of these Nile tantrums with huge losses each time. After trying many defensive tactics, the village gave up and moved to a hilly area not far away from the Nile bank. This saved Artimoga from the famous 1988 Nile flooding.

Life in the village usually goes on at a slow, monotonous tempo. At dawn, men would be seen walking hurriedly to the mosque, women milking the goats to prepare for the early morning tea which would be normally served with homemade pancakes and Ligaimat (doughnuts). Older children would be preparing to go to school located in the neighbouring town. They would gather their books and pencils in the cloth pouch which they strapped across their shoulders, to keep it safe during their long donkey ride to the school. The pouch also contained the child's breakfast, a broad beans sandwich wrapped in an old newspaper and secured by a rubber band.

Younger children with nothing to do, have a lie in. In the afternoon men return from the fields, women get the lunch ready. Children return tired and exhausted from the long day at school and the arduous journey, but still have a few tasks to do before they sit for their lunch. They have to say the Duhr prayer, give the donkey its meal, provide water for the goats and set the table. After lunch, the entire household starts the long-awaited afternoon siesta.

In the evening the children do their homework in the flickering light of an old oil lamp, with the younger siblings trying to make this task as difficult as possible. This usually turns into a mini fight, which comes to a swift conclusion following a stiff stir from dad. After dinner and Isha prayers, the lights are off, and everybody goes to sleep. The village is eerily quiet, except for the barking of stray dogs and braying of a bored donkey. Next day the same cycle is repeated with minor variations.

The whole village, and indeed the whole area, come to life during the dates' harvest season which coincides with the schools' holidays. Dates is one of the main cash crops for northern Sudan and Artimoga is no exception. Those people originally from Artimoga but working in Khartoum and other big cities, usually plan their annual leaves to coincide with the dates' harvest season and to attend the many weddings which take place during that time. Intramarriage is a common tradition, and in some ways an obligation. It is not uncommon, therefore, to find that the whole village shares a similar DNA sequence and genetic orientation. This culture, and deep-rooted tradition has allowed inherited disease conditions to be transmitted from generation to generation. Education and the spread of knowledge started to chip away at the hard rock of this tradition and hopefully it won't be long before we see the back of it, and for good.

There isn't much in the way of entertainment in the village. Children play some games in the fading light of the retreating, late, afternoon sun. The sun always seems to be in a hurry as if it has been chased away by the rapidly advancing darkness of the night. Its face starts to turn red, possibly from that long tiring chase. Beyond the horizon, it plunges down into a mysterious world which it calls home. I suspect the sun goes straight to bed after a long day of hard work, giving warmth and life to all creatures, large and small. Men, on the other hand gather in front of the village shop to discuss serious matters concerning the village, or just have a chat. At Isha prayer time they join those who are already in the mosque.

After the prayer they shuffle back home through the narrow, snaky roads of their village. There is no television, no radio, and no other sort of entertainment. It comes as no surprise that the average number of kids per family is seven. Having a lot of children is important in two respects. One is to balance the high infant mortality rate, and the other as a kind of investment. Boys provide much needed help in the farm, and those clever enough may go all the way to university and get a good job. Part of the salary will find its way to his father as an obligatory contribution to help in the running costs of the big family. Girls usually help in housework from an early age. This is important as they get married very young and from day one, they are expected to run the household, with a little help from their mother. Village girls are lucky to go beyond primary school education. Some forward-thinking fathers who believe in the value of education, allow their daughters to go to secondary school, and even to university. This usually, is not met with approval from the village elders, and sanctions might be imposed on such fathers. These sanctions may take the form of a social boycott, or exclusion from the village decision making process, or any other sanctions they see fit. Some fathers buckle under the heavy weight of these sanctions and remove their daughters from school. Others stand their ground in the belief that the benefit of education far outweighs the village elders' disapproval and what comes with it. The consensus is that girl's education is not that important. At the most, they should have primary education and get married by the time they are fourteen or fifteen. Boys fare a little better compared to girls. The majority goes up to junior secondary school and drops off to help in the farm, or whichever trade the father is engaged in. This is considered as the normal progression of things in the village. The exception is those boys who proceed to university education and beyond. It is, therefore, fair to say that those who are born in the village, grow up in the village, get married in the village and die in the village. Having said that, the arable land is limited and can't support everybody. This forces some young men to leave the village and try their luck somewhere else. They head to big cities where chances for unskilled labour abound. There they usually stay with a relative until they sort themselves out. Staying with a relative with free full board for as long as you want is common practice. It is the extended family system dictate that makes it an obligation for you to play host to your relatives, at any time, and for as long as it takes without uttering a single word of discontent. It is not unusual for a relative to knock on your door in the small hours of the morning, and without prior notice and expect you to welcome him with open arms and a bright smile on your face.

From the time of his arrival, and until he leaves, you must put all your plans on hold and make his a priority. When he, at last leaves, you must buy him a few things and even give him pocket money. Some people factor these expected extra expenses in their budget. This is how the whole society works, and everybody seems to be happy with it.

<hr />

Chapter 2

THE EPIC JOURNEY

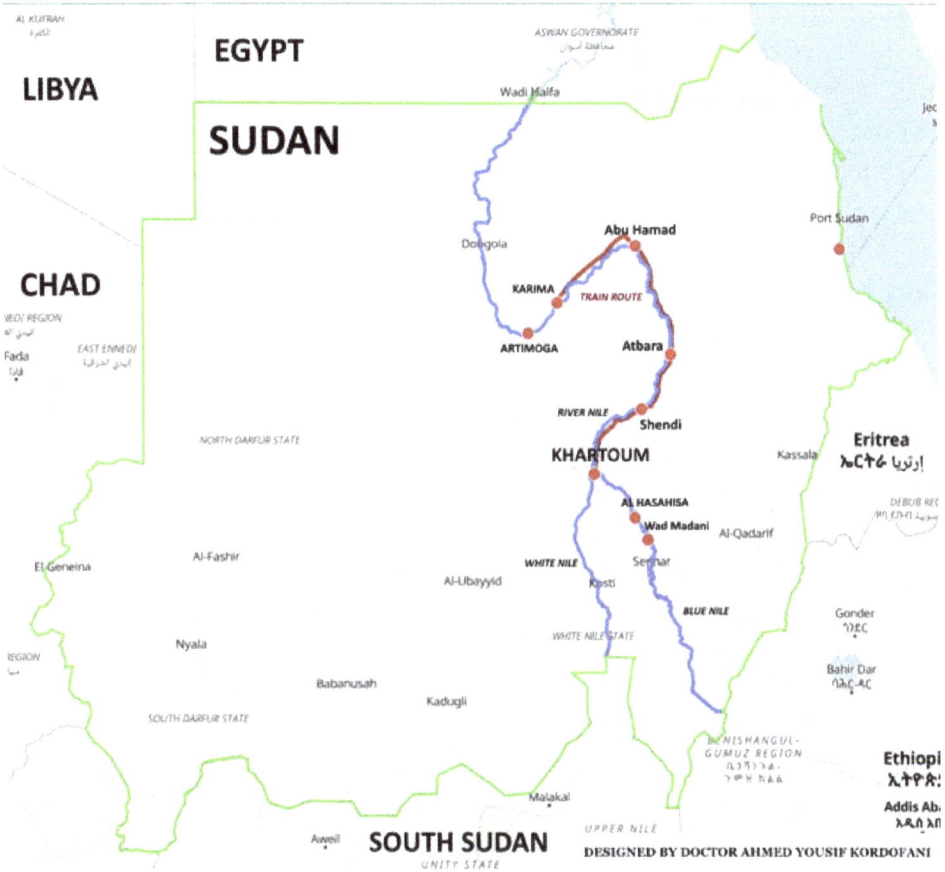

This is a map of Sudan showing the main cities, and the railway line from Karima to Khartoum.

"Courtesy of Dr Ahmed Yousof Alkordofani"

Mr Osman left Artimoga when he was 18 years old. He decided to leave the village as he could see no future for himself there. He could imagine himself forty years down the line working in the family farm, married with a lot of kids, and living a copy paste life of his father and grandfather. He didn't want this. He needed to explore the world and see what is happening beyond the limits of his village. He knew from Geography lessons that there were places far away with big cities, asphalt roads and many cars. But the only way to go to these faraway places is by an aeroplane. The only aeroplane he has seen so far is the one flying high overhead with a trail of smoke behind it, or as a blinking red light in the night sky. Night skies in Artimoga are studded with bright stars, and you can very clearly see the milky way. He always wondered if he will ever be travelling in one of those aeroplanes. He had no idea how big these aeroplanes are or how many people they can carry. He also wondered how they could fly so high, and how they could find their way in this vast expanse of nothing. He strongly believed that these aeroplanes are the making of alien creatures with extraordinary powers. "Oh, I would like to go and live with those aliens and see what other wonderful things they are making," he often whispered to himself. He sat under that palm tree on the bank of the Nile daydreaming about those faraway places, and how those aliens looked like. Were they friendly? Will they accept him? Will they allow him to marry one of their girls? Maybe, he will have children half human and half alien. He laughed at the crazy idea. He had sleepless nights thinking about this, and about how to tell his parents, now that he had decided to leave his beloved Artimoga. It seemed to him that now is the right time. He sat with his father with the intention of breaking the news of his decision to him, but somehow convinced himself that his father was not in a good mood, and it was better to tell him another time. This "another" time came one Friday.

"Dad, I have decided to go to Khartoum to work there."

"So, you have already decided?"

"Yes"

"Tell me about your plans. You must have made some plans."

"Will take the train and go to stay with uncle Ahmed."

"*Did you tell him?*"

"*He already knows but asked me to tell you first. He promised to find a job there.*"

"*Did he tell you what kind of job?*"

"*He knows someone who will help me join the police force.*"

"*That is good I suppose. How much is the salary?*"

"*He did not say. He told me it is a good salary, good enough for you to send money to your father.*"

"*Oh!*"

"*Do you have the money for the train ticket?*"

"*Yes.*"

"*We better tell your mother then.*"

His mum was sad that he was leaving, but happy for him as that was what he wanted to do. He promised that he would write to them regularly and come home on holidays. The news spread like wildfire, and the entire village came to their house to say their farewell and wish him all the best. Everyone was happy for him. May be one girl was not that happy; in fact, she was angry and worried. Being his cousin, she was pencilled to be his future wife. But now he was going to Khartoum where girls are sophisticated, and they know how to lure men and captivate their hearts, she was not sure anymore. She clearly remembered her neighbour Hassan, who went to Khartoum, and one year later he got married to a Khartoum girl, ditching his fiancée in Artimoga She felt some pain in her heart, and a teardrop skimmed down her left cheek. She quickly chased these thoughts out of her head. Now she was saying to herself, "Osman will go to Khartoum and start a job with a good salary, save a lot of money, come back, and marry her and host a wedding party; Artimoga would have never seen anything like it before. He will take her with him to Khartoum. All the village girls will envy her." She was awakened from her daydreaming by the screaming voice of her mother. "Don't stand there like a zombie, go and milk the goat and prepare milk for Mohamed (her two-year-old brother)." This brought her to earth with a sobering thud. That night she couldn't sleep, wondering how the farewell was going to be? Will

Osman say anything to her? Will he come around to her house to say goodbye? Will he promise her anything?

At dawn Osman took the bus to catch the early morning train from Karima to Khartoum, the advice of his father ringing in his ears, and his mother's mumbling of some prayers, mixed with audible sobbing sank deep into his soul. It was January, and it was bitterly cold at that time of the morning. All the passengers were well wrapped up, you could see only their eyes, whose pupils were fully dilated but still couldn't see much as it was still pitch dark. The passengers sat silently in their seats while the bus rumbled along a dirt track littered with potholes.

They arrived at Karima railway station and were welcomed by a loud hoot from the steam engine train. Osman took his tin suitcase and headed for the train. It contained two Jalabiyas, three shirts and a five years' old pair of trousers that he inherited from his cousin. His mother added two egg sandwiches and some dry dates for him to eat during his thirty hours' journey. The tin suitcase was secured with a huge padlock, which any piece of wire could unlock, but still gave a sense of invincibility, and acted as a deterrent to thieves by virtue of its size.

He sat in a fourth-class cabin on a wooden bench and put his tin suitcase on his lap. It contained all his material possessions, and he must take utmost care of it. It wasn't long before the train slowly and reluctantly pulled out of the station announcing its departure with a loud, high pitched and prolonged hoot, and a cloud of thick, black smoke bellowing out of its upturned nostril. It headed northeast following the obtuse bend of the Nile as if it was afraid to lose its way travelling across the desert. Following the Nile would almost double its journey in distance and duration, but again most people lived along the Nile bank.

Osman never knew that trains, or anything for that matter, could travel that fast. Telephone posts travelled so fast in the opposite direction, making it impossible for him to count them so he gave up. He never left his seat, and his tin suitcase never left his lap. His legs felt numb, and he felt that he needed to eat something. He carefully opened his suitcase and took out one egg sandwich and five dry dates. He then locked the suitcase. The passenger next to him must have wondered what was in that case for it to be locked with such a huge padlock. Osman started eating his sandwich gazing aimlessly out of the carriage window. He suddenly realized that the objects nearer to the train travelled backwards, while those farthest away travelled in the same direction as the train. He quickly realized that the explanation was beyond him. He finished eating the egg sandwich and dates and nodded off. His bladder woke him up, asking him to get up and go to the toilet. Now? While the train is moving? No way!

The ticket conductor came around to check the tickets. Osman handed him his and asked him hesitantly when train was going to stop next. "In fifteen minutes" came the answer. The fifteen minutes felt like ages before the train came to a halt. The station was a tiny one, in the middle of nowhere. Few houses were scattered randomly around the track, but not a soul to be seen apart from the station officials. Wondering what to do with his suitcase when he disembarked, he decided to ask the passenger next to him to look after it.

"Where are you going?" asked the passenger.

"I am disembarking to go and urinate."

"The train will be stopping for a couple of minutes only. Why can't you use the toilets on the train?"

"Toilets on the train?" he exclaimed with a hint of disbelief.

"Yes. You see that door over there? That is the toilet. But you can use it only after the train pulls out of the station."

After the train pulled out of the station and gathered speed, he opened the toilet door, not having the foggiest idea what the toilet would look like inside. It was a small room with a wash basin, a hole in the floor and a jug of water presumably to wash your bum with. He looked down the hole and immediately felt dizzy as the ground was racing backwards. He closed his eyes, but this affected his aim causing the urine stream trajectory to miss the intended hole and splash all over the place. Relieved but still feeling dizzy, he washed his hands and went back to his seat. The train stopped at many small stations to pick up a couple of passengers and drop a few.

Late evening it stopped at a huge station, huge by Osman's standards. It had many dazzling bright lights, cafes and restaurants and a bustling market. Most of the passengers disembarked, but Osman remained rooted to his seat to look after his suitcase. He also didn't have enough money to spend, and things in this big city must be very expensive compared to Artimoga. He carefully took out an egg sandwich and few dates for his dinner and started munching. He finished eating, wiped his mouth with the back of his left hand, flung his head back and hoped he could sleep. Suddenly doubt crept into his mind and he started to wonder if he had taken the right decision leaving the place he knew very well, for the unknown. Why couldn't he live like his father and grandfather who spent all their lives in Artimoga, living a happy and peaceful life. What if he is unable to make it in Khartoum. Would Artimoga accept him back after he betrayed her. Was his mother happy for him? Why was she crying so much? Was he going to see her ever again? He felt homesick already. These thoughts chased sleep away. Now he was wide awake gazing into the vast darkness enveloping the horizon and beyond, but oblivious to the other passengers who were chatting and laughing loudly. Could it be possible that these passengers had no worries or problems bothering them? Or might be they were laughing to forget them, even if temporarily. Maybe he should do the same, he said to himself. Looking at the darkness he suddenly realized that the darker it becomes, the closer it will be to dawn and brightness. This thought brought him some peace of mind and some comfort and convinced him that things would be fine. He felt sleepy, and before long he was dozing off, helped by the rhythmic movements of the train and the orchestrated sounds of its wheels on the track. Soon he was fast asleep but still holding on to his suitcase on his lap. Most of the passengers were sleeping or preparing to do so. That passenger next to him kept looking at the huge padlock, and wondered, "What was in that suitcase for it to be locked with such a huge padlock, and never to leave its owner's lap and his clutches?" Osman didn't look like a rich man and the fact that he was travelling in the fourth-class carriage proved it. The suitcase itself was old and cheap but could all this be a clever camouflage? "This is not any of my business." he said to himself, but still curiosity was killing him, and he was itching to solve that riddle. *Might be he should ask this passenger a direct question when he woke up in the morning.*

While he was trying to find a nice formulation for the question, he remembered that on his first ever train trip he did the same as this passenger. Although his padlock was not as big as this, his suitcase never left his lap. He even took it with him to the toilet. His friends told him then that the train was full of thieves, and he must be careful with his possessions. So, the solution to this riddle was simple. This is the first time that this passenger had set foot on a train. He smiled to himself with much satisfaction and felt capable of solving any riddle no matter how complicated it was. He looked around the carriage and realized that he was the only one who was still awake. He shifted a little in his seat, used his right arm as a pillow, closed his eyes and begged sleep to take control. Sleep obliged and he soon found himself wandering in the world of dreams and false reality.

The passengers were rudely awakened by the conductor knocking loudly on the side of the carriage. It was around five in the morning. Some passengers continued their sleep, but the majority were clumsily searching their pockets for the tickets while silently cursing the conductor. Those still asleep, or pretending to be, were unceremoniously woken up by the conductor slapping them on the cheek and pulling them up into a sitting position. One of the passengers was fined on the spot for travelling on the train without a ticket. The conductor did not even listen to his excuses. He paid the fine without argument, persuaded by a stern look from the police officer accompanying the conductor. He was still mumbling something, long after the conductor was gone. He had a ticket but couldn't find it, and the conductor wouldn't give him time to look for it. The conductor saw and checked his ticket the first time around but of course did not remember because of the sheer number of passengers. He looked everywhere but couldn't find the damn ticket. He looked at the latest passenger who joined the carriage with some suspicion. He seemed a bit nervous when he handed his ticket to the conductor, and afterwards he went and sat at the far end of the carriage, keeping to himself.

Just before sunrise the train pulled into a relatively large station with a sigh of relief in the form of a tired hoot, and at the same time coughing up some thick black smoke as if trying to clear its steel throat. The sun peeped, from behind the horizon as a glowing red ball rising slowly, but steadily into the sky giving warmth and chasing the cold weather away. The doors of the carriages were flung open, and the passengers poured out. They hurried in a shuffling gait across a sandy square towards the area where cafes and restaurants were located.

However, they headed straight to a small mosque, past the restaurants, to say their morning prayers. Saying prayers came first. Although it was still early in the morning all the restaurants and cafés were open and ready to welcome customers. The passengers infused life into the restaurants. Now all the tables were occupied, waiters shouting orders to the chef in a loud voice and informing the teller what the customer standing in front of him should pay. How they remembered that, only God knew. Customers were understandably inpatient as the train halted there for around thirty minutes only. In this short time, they needed to pray, have their meal and a cup of tea or coffee. Waiters were having a hard time as every customer wanted to be attended to first. Waiters somehow made everybody think that he was the next to be served. In the end all were happy. The customers were fed and had water, waiters were satisfied with a job well done and the restaurant owners' kitty was full of money.

Osman didn't leave his seat. He couldn't figure out what to do with the suitcase. He thought it would be odd to carry it with him as he noticed that no one was doing that. He also considered those who left their suitcases behind were careless, and he was not going to be one of them. He felt uncomfortable sitting all by himself. The passenger sitting next to him walked in.

"Alsalam alaikum!"

"Wa alaikum Alsalem!"

"Where are you from?"

"Artimoga."

"I am from Ganati."

"Oh! Do you know my uncle Salah. He lives in Ganati, he owns a corner shop there."

"No, I am sorry I don't know him, but I must have seen him or been to his shop."

"He is famous there. He is very rich. Has two wives and many kids."

"I am from Ganati alright, but I live in Khartoum and go to Ganati only on holidays."

"That restaurant in the corner has very nice food. In which restaurant did you eat?"

"I ate an egg sandwich here. I didn't leave the train."

"Didn't leave the train!! Why?"

"Just didn't feel like it."

"Is this your first train trip?"

"Yes. I never left Artimoga before."

"Do you want me to get you anything?"

"No, but thank you all the same."

"Are you going to Khartoum?"

"Yes."

"Do you have relatives there?"

"Yes."

"Are you going there to work or just visiting?"

"To work"

"Where?"

Osman got fed up with this interrogation and wondered why this guy was asking him all these questions. He got up and headed towards the toilet accompanied by his suitcase. No way he was going to leave his suitcase behind. He must be careful of this guy; he was up to no good. Coming out of the toilet, he surveyed the carriage for empty seats. To his disappointment there were no vacant seats apart from his. He reluctantly trotted back to his seat to a welcoming smile from his annoying neighbour.

"Is your relative going to meet you at the station?"

"Yes."

"What would you do if he doesn't come?"

"He will come."

With this, Osman looked out of the window and started watching passengers hurriedly to-ing and fro-ing trying to get all the things they needed before the train departed. His neighbour asked yet another question, but he ignored him.

Thirty seconds after a loud whistle, the train wheels started to turn pulling the train out of the station. It quickly gathered speed belching thick smoke and coughing like a heavy smoker. Now the station appeared as an insignificant something below the horizon. Only the tall white minaret of the mosque could be seen clearly. The track was now very close to the Nile bank. You could not miss the distinctive smell of the Nile and its refreshing breath. Osman closed his eyes to enjoy the moment. A flock of birds, in a military like formation, were flying effortlessly just inches above the surface of the water, and only a few meters from a fisherman on his boat, hoping for a good catch. The rays of the early morning sun bounced off the mirror-like surface of the water flooding it with a shimmering light. Slender branches were trying hard to reach the water and kiss it good morning, while bigger branches were having an early morning dip. A couple of dragon flies were engaged in a beautiful mating, water skiing dance oblivious to the dangers lurking underneath. A floating dry leaf was used by a clever beetle as an effortless mode of transport. A bright yellow flower seemed to be admiring her beautiful reflection in the water, to the envy of pale flowers around it.

Osman could not see all this from where he was sitting but could imagine it. After all, he lived all his life by the Nile bank and had seen similar scenes many times over.

The train parted company with the Nile, passing near many scattered villages, stopping at some and ignoring others. Khartoum was now three hours away. The conductor came around for his final ticket checking. This time he passed through the carriage surveying the passengers. He didn't inspect any tickets after realizing that there were no newcomers. He responded to one of the passengers that the *train would be arriving in Khartoum on time, at seven in the evening. Osman's heart missed a beat. He would soon be arriving in Khartoum. What would the place be like? Would his uncle remember to come and meet him? What would he do if, for any reason his uncle didn't come? He had no idea in which part of Khartoum his uncle lived. If his uncle didn't come, he was doomed. He felt some cold sweat on his forehead and down his arm pits. An overwhelming feeling of worry and panic swept over him. His thoughts shifted back to Artimoga and to his parents and siblings. Would he ever see them again?*

"Get ready, we will soon be arriving in Khartoum." That passenger said to him, interrupting his thoughts.

"I am ready."

"Where does your uncle live?"

"In Khartoum."

"Which area? "

"I don't know. Why are you asking?"

"My brother is a taxi driver. He can give you a lift if your uncle lives in the same area."

"That's very kind of you."

"Also, my brother knows a lot of people in Khartoum, and he might help fix you a job."

"That will be good. I need to find a job as quickly as possible. I don't like sitting around doing nothing."

"Oh, don't you worry there are a lot of jobs in Khartoum. You will be spoilt for choice."

Osman started to like this guy. He seemed to be willingly helpful, but still reminded himself to be careful and not to trust strangers too much.

"That's Khartoum. Those distant lights. We are almost there."

⟡

Abdelrahman Abdalaziz

Chapter 3

THE BIG CITY

Wide eyed and with his jaw dropping, Osman looked in amazement at the explosion of lights as the train rumbled through the outskirts of Khartoum. He had never seen anything like it before. He wondered where they find enough oil for all these lamps. Also, it must take them a long time to light the lamps, and to put the lights off. Surely, they needed to employ many people to do this. He could easily do such a job. He was the one responsible for the oil lamps of the mosque in Artimoga, and surely these ones were no different. He noticed that these lamps were a lot brighter than those in Artimoga and somewhat different in shape. Some were blue, some red, some blinking, some going around in circles and some in the form of words. That was crazy. These lamps were different and beyond his ability to deal with them. One job opportunity gone.

The train crossed a river over a steel bridge which shock under the weight of the train. Now the train was slowing down to a jogging pace. Osman could see things in more detail. Tall buildings with many windows. It must be a struggle to go to the top floor, Osman concluded. Lots of cars and buses speeding along black smooth, well-lit, and tree-lined roads. Smartly dressed pedestrians were walking on the pavement.

Finally, the train came to a halt at Khartoum main railway station, announcing its arrival with a tired whistle. There was a large welcoming crowd. Passengers poured out of the train, some received by their waiting relatives or friends while others headed straight to the taxi stand or the bus stop outside the station. Osman anxiously scanned the crowd for his uncle whom he last saw about three years ago. He is not sure if he would be able to recognise him.

"Is your uncle here yet?" Asked that passenger who was sitting next to him in the carriage, and at the same time introduced his brother, the taxi driver.

"I can't see him yet, but I am sure he is here. Too many people."

"OK we will wait."

An anxious twenty minutes passed and still his uncle didn't show up.

A gentle tap on the shoulder, and his uncle was there behind him with open arms and a big smile on his face. For the first time Osman let go of his tin suitcase and hugged his uncle. What a relief!

"Where about in Khartoum do you live?"

"In Jabra."

"I live there too. Come on I will give you lift."

"Thank you very much indeed."

During the thirty minutes journey Osman was quiet. Everything was strange and overwhelming and difficult to take in. Lights everywhere. Hundreds of cars, many of them were yellow, moving very fast. Now his head was spinning, and he was not sure if this was a dream or reality.

The taxi stopped in front of an indistinct, mid-terrace house with jaundiced walls. Osman noticed that the houses were painted in different colours but most of the front doors were blue. Was this by choice or design, he asked himself. The taxi driver got down and took the tin suitcase out of the boot.

"We live three streets away," announced the taxi driver.

"Oh really?" exclaimed Osman's uncle.

"We are almost neighbours. Our paths must have crossed before. Please do come and visit us sometime, both of you. Consider this as an invitation. Thank you again for the lift."

"You are welcome. Goodbye."

They drove off along the dirt road with a trail of dust chasing them.

Osman silently followed his uncle into the house. The old door opened with a loud squeak betraying its arthritic hinges. The door lead into a mini garden with two mango trees, one lemon tree and three date palms. The house itself was a one storey building with three bedrooms and a kitchen opening into a generous veranda. There was an annexe attached to the house where guests could stay. It was also used to receive male visitors.

His wife, Zainab, was a plump lady of average height and pale complexion. She warmly welcomed Osman and offered him a glass of cold lemon juice.

"Where are the twins?"

"They are in their room doing their homework."

"Ask them to come and say hello to their cousin."

Ten years old Hashim and Hisham came darting out of their room to this welcome break from the boredom of homework. They were identical twins and it was impossible to know who is who. They very often used this similarity to play games on their parents and teachers. They had never seen Osman before. They chatted with him briefly, and by dad's orders reluctantly went to their room to finish the homework. There were three other younger siblings, two girls and a boy. They were already in their room ready for bed.

Osman was taken to the annexe and shown where he was going to stay. A bare room devoid of any furniture apart from two single beds and a small rickety table. Three nails in the wall presumably for hanging clothes.

"Get changed and rest a little bit. We will be having dinner soon." This sounded like music to Osman's ears. For the last day and a half, he had lived on three egg sandwiches and a few dates. He was starving. He pushed his tin suitcase under the bed and laid down with his legs dangling by the side. He kept looking at the light bulb and wondering how it emitted the light. In the end he gave up. Hunger pangs were affecting his power to think. Now all his senses were on high alert for any sign of "dinner is served." He waited. Kept looking, listening, and smelling.

A gentle knock, and his uncle came into the room and broke the good news. Dinner was ready. He followed his uncle into a small *dining area next to the kitchen. On a small dining table lay a round tray covered with what looked like a large Mexican hat. Osman's nose picked the unmistakable smell of roast chicken. His stomach rumbled with expectations. The Mexican hat was removed, and there it was. A big roasted whole chicken occupying the centre of the tray surrounded by curry dishes, rice, soup, green salad and of course, bread. Osman ate until his stomach could take no more. He left no space for water, and he could hardly breathe. The tray was taken away and another one brought in. Baklava, a bowl of fruit salad and tea. He liked desert but could eat only a little bit of it. He couldn't summon the courage to ask Zainab to put some away for him.*

Chapter 4

THE DISAPPOINTMENT

*O*ver dinner his uncle confirmed that the job in the police force was guaranteed. Osman needed to attend an interview at the police force headquarters the next day. This interview was just a formality, and the job was his. His uncle would take him there in the morning.

"Now you go and say your prayers and go to bed. We need to be there at 7am for the interview. Punctuality is very important in the police force, and you must make a good, first impression. Also, you must dress well and appear confident."

"What will they ask about?"

"Just a general chat in your case. Then you will undergo a medical examination to make sure you are fit for the job."

"Medical examination?"

"A doctor will ask you a few questions, examine you and do some blood tests and X-Rays."

"That's fine," Osman replied nervously. He had needle phobia. He started perspiring.

"Good night. We will set off at six, inshallah."

Osman didn't sleep a wink all night. His stomach was too full, he was worried about the interview and above all, the blood test. By five thirty he was up and ready. They had tea with some cakes and left the house at six. The police headquarters was a grand, three storeyed, blue building. Inside, policemen of different ranks, in blue immaculate uniforms were walking upright and briskly, and saluting each other.

They waited in front of an office and before long, Osman was called in. He received a reassuring look from his uncle before going into the office. Two officers with a lot of brass on their shoulders were sitting at an oval table with two steaming, coffee mugs. Osman sat on a chair at the instruction of one of the officers.

They asked him a few general questions about himself and why he wanted to be a policeman. The whole episode took a little more than five minutes. Osman thought they wanted to enjoy their coffee before it got cold. They asked him to wait in front of the office where somebody would come and take him to do the medical tests. He told his uncle what happened. His uncle didn't say anything, as if he knew already.

A tall, lanky guy introduced himself as officer Sharif, and asked Osman to follow him. Sharif walked so quickly Osman had to jog to keep pace with him. They arrived at a separate, two storeyed building, presumably the medical centre. The lady at the reception desk took his details on a busy form capturing every detail of his life, his family, and his political orientation.

In another room his weight, height, blood pressure, pulse and temperature were recorded. Then he was taken to another room full of funny looking machines where eye tests were done. A long printout came out of one of the machines on which the technician wrote some comments and handed to officer Sharif. Officer Sharif glanced at the report and asked Osman to follow him. They headed back to where they came from. Osman was very happy because no blood tests were done. After a gentle knock on the door and an authoritative "come in" officer Sharif went in and closed the door behind him, while Osman waited outside with his uncle. A few minutes later Osman was invited in.

"You performed very well in the interview but unfortunately the tests showed that you suffer from colour blindness, and as such I am afraid, we cannot select you to work in the police force. I am sure you will find a suitable job, and I wish you all the best."

Osman couldn't believe his ears. Colour blind? How come he was not aware of it. He just stood there; his eyes wide open but seeing nothing, like someone in a trance. All his senses were numb.

"That's all. You can go."

Still shocked, he exited the office and immediately broke the bad news to his uncle. His uncle was very upset and angry. These people promised him that Osman will get this job. Who cares about the difference between violet and purple or the different shades of green? What has this to do with being a policeman? Bastards! Now he had to sort out another job for him, and quick.

On the way home Osman remembered what his fellow passenger said about his brother, the taxi driver, but kept the thought to himself. His uncle was quiet but fuming inside, still not believing what had just happened. He had no plan B for Osman. He needed to start from scratch to find a job for him. This would take time and effort. Worse still he might not be able to.

Zainab opened the door for them. They went straight to the annex after asking her to make something light to eat and some tea. From their body language Zainab knew that something was amiss. They sat looking at each other as if saying "so what is next?" Zainab brought the food and tea. They started eating, but the food did not taste the same. Even their taste buds were not happy.

"You know that taxi driver who gave us a lift?"

"Yes. What about him?"

"His brother told me that he knows a lot of people and can help me find a job. Can you talk to him?
"

"I will do. I need to go to work now. Have a look at the garden and, as a farmer, see if anything needs to be done. These mature mango trees haven't borne fruits yet."

"Will see what I can do," Osman replied vacantly.

"You need to write a letter to your parents, for them to know that you arrived here safely and in one piece."

"Shall I tell them about what happened today?"

"No."

His uncle hurriedly left the house. Osman lay on the bed contemplating what to say to his parents. He would tell them that he was fine and would soon find a job. He would also add a brief description of Khartoum as he saw it so far. He felt sleepy due to lack of sleep the night before, so he decided to take a nap. He kept tossing and turning for a while before he finally settled down into a rapid eye movement sleep. He was woken up by one of the twins (difficult to say who), still in his school uniform, telling him that his uncle had come back from work, and lunch would be served soon. He got up, washed, and said his Duhr prayer. He went to the dining area and sat without uttering a word. His uncle was already at the table, reading a newspaper.

After lunch, the entire household settled into a long, afternoon siesta. There is a strong belief that after lunch you have to rest, and after dinner you go for a stroll, something which is believed to be good for your health. The origin of this belief was not known, and its benefit has never been proven. Most probably it is just a habit, a bad habit, and people are trying to find some justification for it.

The twins woke up first, as they had some homework to do, and after that a football training session. They took their football very seriously. Nothing made them miss a training session. The coach could see the potential in them and was determined to make something out of them. They were vital members of the school's first football team. They won the school tournament for two years in a row and now they were the defending champions. Although it was too early to say, the coach was predicting that both would one day be playing professionally for one of the local teams, and who knows, may be for the country.

Osman started writing a letter to his parents. It was a short letter. He basically told them that he arrived safely, and the prospects of finding a job were high. He also gave them a brief account of what he saw of Khartoum. He put the letter in an envelope, on which he wrote his father's name. The postman would be anyone travelling to Artimoga, who was going to hand deliver it to his father. Even parcels and packages were posted the same way. There was no postal service, as such, to Artimoga. Official governmental post was carried by train to Karima, and then by road in a governmental car to Artimoga. This activity was done only once a week.

At five o'clock, Osman and his uncle sat for the evening tea which was normally taken with some home baked cakes. The discussion was all about finding a job for Osman. His uncle was going to contact some of his friends to see if they could help, but deep down he was not optimistic. Somehow, Osman could read his uncle's thoughts and that made him depressed.

The twins and one of the younger siblings came and started chatting with their father. They wanted some money to buy ice cream from the ice cream van which announced its arrival at the end of their street with a loud, badly composed musical piece. The children grabbed some money and shot out of the house, leaving their father mumbling, "this ice cream van should be banned."

Chapter 5

THE TURN OF FORTUNE

*A*car stopped outside and there was a knock on the door. Osman answered the door. There was a taxi, and the taxi driver who gave them a lift from the railway station. A strange feeling went through Osman, a nice feeling. He couldn't explain it but who cared, a nice feeling was a nice feeling.

"Alsalamualaikum!"

"Wa alaikum alsalam!"

"Is your uncle in?"

"Yes. Please come in."

"I am Omer. I am sure you remember me."

"Of course, I do. Come on, man, my memory is not that bad," Osman's uncle replied jokingly.

"I came to invite you both to have dinner at my house this Friday. I hope you will be able to come."

"I think this Friday is ok. Thank you for the invite."

"Great. See you next Friday, inshallah."

With this the taxi driver got up, and started walking towards the door, apologizing that he could not stay long as he had some urgent business to attend to. At the door he paused and turned around.

"By the way, a friend of mine wants a shop assistant urgently. He is a big businessman owning many shops. He needs somebody who is honest, reliable, and hard working. Would you be interested, Osman? If you are, then I will take you to meet him the day after tomorrow."

Osman couldn't believe what he had just heard.

"Yes, I am very interested. I haven't worked in a shop before, but I am definitely honest, reliable and hard working."

"Don't worry, you seem to be a fast learner."

"What kind of stuff does he trade in".

"He has many shops and is involved in different kinds of trade. You will see when you meet him. I can tell you now that the job is yours. I will come around the day after tomorrow, at nine in the morning. See you then."

Osman and his uncle were cautiously optimistic after their recent disappointment at the police headquarters. There were no plans for celebrations yet. They would believe it, only when it was in the bag.

"What do you think the salary will be," asked Osman.

"Let us wait to meet the man and see the place, you might not like it."

"Like it or not, I will take it. It is better than being without a job. I can always leave for a better one."

"I agree."

"By the way I wrote a letter to my father. Do you think, before sending it, I should wait till we know the outcome of this job?"

"Yes, it is a good idea. Hopefully you will add some good news," his uncle remarked with a wink. Osman grinned, but said nothing.

That evening Osman lay on his bed, fully clothed, and drifted into daydreaming. He had lots of money, a big house, and a car, got married to a beautiful girl and .... This stream of unreality was interrupted by summons to dinner.

The journey to meet the prospective employer took around forty-five minutes. All the way Osman was silent, listening to the taxi driver singing the praises of this businessman. They arrived at a pale yellow, three storeyed building with a big sign above the entrance saying in bold black letters "The rising sun enterprises." The entrance led into a foyer with a reception desk at the left-hand corner. The desk was manned by an elegantly dressed young woman with a welcoming smile.

"Salamualaikum Mr Khalid. How can I help"?

"Wa alaikum alsalam Sara. Can we see the boss?"

"He has a meeting in half an hour; I will see if he can see you in the meantime." She picked up the phone and whispered something, replaced the receiver, and asked them to go to the office on the first floor.

"Do you know where the office is?"

"Of course, I do. I am a kind of a part time employee. I know everyone here; I know the big boss himself. He is my classmate, and we were very close school friends. He inherited a lot of money which he managed very well, creating a very successful business empire."

"What kind of a man is he?"

"You will see, you will see."

At the top of the stairs, they turned right, along a corridor at the end of which there was an office with the sign "General Manager" on its door. Khalid paused at the door, turned to Osman and said, "Just be yourself." Khalid rang the bell and seconds later the door opened. They went into a beautifully decorated office with a secretary at the desk.

"Hi Mr Khalid, nice to see you," she greeted him with an obvious familiarity, got up and walked to a door, closely followed by Osman's gaze. She was wearing a short, tight, black dress which didn't leave much to the imagination, black shoes with very high heels. Osman wondered how she was able to keep her balance. She reappeared at the door and ushered them in.

They entered into a big office with two glass windows, and its walls painted sky blue. On one side there was an oval table with a dozen chairs around it. On the other side there was a huge mahogany desk with fat legs and two armchairs in front of it. Behind the desk sat a well-built, middle-aged man with grey hair at the temples. He stood up, greeted them warmly and invited them to have a seat.

"This is Osman, the guy I told you about. He is keen to work for you."

"I understood from Khalid that you just arrived from Artimoga, and this is your first visit to Khartoum."

"Yes, that is right."

"I need somebody to work in one of my stores in Khartoum. The job is easy to learn, someone will be your mentor and show you the ropes. I need somebody who is honest and hardworking. You will work six days a week. Your accommodation is free. You will be living with other employees in a flat just above the store. Your salary is twenty-two pounds per month. Go and think about it and let me know your decision by tomorrow. Sorry to push you but I need to close this issue."

"I can tell you now that I accept the job offer and can start any time. I assure you that I am an honest person and will work hard to do a good job."

"That's fine then. Go to the secretary, she will tell you what to do next and make you sign the contract."

Osman thanked him and went out of the office with a big smile on his face. He could not wait to tell his uncle and add this piece of good news to the letter he had written to his father.

The secretary handed him the contract which he signed without reading.

"Bring your stuff to the flat next Thursday and your first working day will be the following Saturday. Your mentor will meet you there and brief you on your job description."

"I don't know where the flat is."

"Don't you worry, I will take you there," Khalid interjected.

"Do you have any questions?' asked the secretary. Osman was not paying attention as he was concentrating on her long, thick eyelashes and wondering how she could see through them.

Khalid gave Osman a lift home and promised to come by in the evening. Osman went straight to the annex, took out the letter and added a paragraph about what had happened today with excitement exuding from the tip of the pen. He could see his father's face lighting up with joy and relief on reading the added paragraph. He put his meagre possessions in the tin suitcase but didn't bother to lock it with that huge padlock. He was ready to go, he couldn't wait.

The Man Who Lost His Face

Chapter 6

THE JOB

*T*he accommodation was a two-bedroom flat; the rooms were of a decent size and each room had two beds and a small old cupboard. From the look of it, tenants had to provide their own bed sheets and pillows. The flat had a basic kitchen, a sitting room, and a bathroom. Two men, sharing one room, worked in the security department. The other was empty. The previous occupant had moved out three days ago. Osman would have this room all to himself, for the moment. Unusual for bachelors, the kitchen was well kept. Osman put his tin suitcase in the cupboard and went to the store to meet his mentor.

The store was a huge one filled up to the ceiling with rows upon rows of different kinds of merchandise. There was a small office, a small coffee room and a toilet.

Beehive activity with a large number of noisy workers. Some were bringing boxes in and some taking boxes out, forklifts lifting things onto shelves or bringing them down. Osman was impressed by the sheer volume of work being done and the way it was being carried out.

The mentor was a tall guy in his fifties with a big moustache and a small chin. The word smile was not in his vocabulary. He introduced himself as Musa, the one in charge there. He took Osman for a tour around the place explaining how the system worked.

"You are going to work in one section where your job is to log things coming in and going out. Also, you need to help in moving and rearranging boxes. Sometimes you might need to help in other sections. It is hard work, but the pay is good. Hard work and honesty, that is what we are looking for. Work runs smoothly here and there is no place for troublemakers." He said all this without looking at Osman even once. He showed Osman how to do the entry in the book and how

41

to make sure that it tallied with the available merchandise at the end of each day.

"I will be helping you for the first two days."

"Thank you."

"Don't thank me, this is my job. You have to pay attention all the time; I don't like saying things twice."

"Ok sir."

"See you on Saturday at 8am on the dot."

Osman went back to the flat, lay on the bare mattress and tried to take in all that had happened. Things had developed at a dizzying pace, but all in the right direction. Now he was employed with a good salary and soon, could start sending money to his family. He had free accommodation next door to his place of work, alhamdullilah. He was very happy, but his happiness was tinged with some sadness as he was missing Artimoga and his family.

Later that day his uncle visited him. He brought bed sheets, a pillow, a plate, a mug and, a spoon, teabags, and sugar. He also gave him five pounds which Osman insisted on it to be considered as a loan which he would pay from his first salary.

Osman worked hard the whole week and on Fridays he went to his uncle's place. Now he could use the public transport to go places. On some Fridays he went with his friends to a café to play cards and backgammon, but by 9 p.m. he had to be back at the flat. For nine months now he worked very hard and did not put a foot wrong. His documentation was perfect and there were no discrepancies between the ins and outs which used to happen before. Stock was moving smoothly, and all the customers were happy and mentioned that to the big boss. Osman was very popular amongst the staff and well-liked by all. That didn't come as a surprise as he was well mannered and very helpful. One day a worker collapsed, and Osman was the one who attended to him and was quick to call the ambulance. He was acting as the team leader who orchestrated the whole first aid operation. This gained him the respect and admiration of his fellow workers. They trusted him and confided in him. They came to him with their personal problems, and usually accepted his suggestions and judgement. He set up a system for them whereby they would purchase food stuff in bulk at wholesale prices and share it. This saved them a lot of money, something they really appreciated. Osman injected a new life in the store, workers were happier as they felt they were well looked after, and now they had a sense of ownership. They treated the store as their own.

One day, the big boss came into the store. This was very unusual. He went into the office and locked the door. What was going on? This was the question on everyone's mind, but they carried on working as usual. An hour or so later, Osman was summoned to the office. His heart started racing and he felt sick. "What did I do wrong?" he wondered, but nothing obvious came to mind.

He knocked on the door with a trembling hand and was allowed in.

"Salamualaikum Osman."

"Walaikum Alsalam boss."

"For the last hour or so I have been looking at your documentation which is absolutely perfect. I have received positive feedback from my customers and from the shop floor. The store is running a lot smoother than before. I have therefore decided to promote you to store supervisor with immediate effect. I will announce this now to the shop floor and you will receive an official letter to that effect."

Osman was speechless. His tongue went stiff, and words just wouldn't come out. The boss went out of the office and Osman followed.

"From this moment Osman will be the store supervisor and will be reporting directly to me. I am sure you will offer him your full support. Now go back to work." There was a loud cheer and clapping from the workers. The boss smiled, convinced by the workers' reaction, that he had made the right decision. The boss then left the store. The workers congratulated Osman and started calling him the little boss. They pledged to work even harder now that he was their boss.

The official letter stipulated that Osman's salary would be raised to thirty-one pounds and he would attend the monthly senior management team meetings held in the company headquarters in downtown Khartoum. He would be provided with company transport if he chose to leave his present accommodation.

He started working only nine months ago and now he was the boss of the store and a member of the senior management team. What a meteoric rise! Will he be the big boss in a couple of years? He wondered. "No, I must set up my own company and be my own boss," he thought to himself. The company will be a big and famous one employing hundreds of people, some of course, from Artimoga. It would be a haulage company transporting goods from Port Sudan to all parts of the country, with hundreds of trucks and containers carrying the name of the company. It would have offices in all major cities. He would call it Artimoga Movers. He was dead serious about it.

In the fourth senior management meeting, Osman attended, it was suggested to open a factory outlet in Hasahisa, in Aljazeera province 140 miles south of Khartoum. To Osman's surprise, he was chosen to manage the project. It was suggested to rent a place there but later they came round to Osman's idea to buy a piece of land in a suitable location and build a retail shop with a wholesale part, and an adjoining big storage compound. The wholesale part would be the distribution centre for the areas south of Khartoum. Such centres would be replicated in other parts of the country.

The following week Osman travelled to Hasahisa to have a feeling of the place. He liked what he saw. A good-sized plot of land in a prime location which would also accommodate a parking area for customers, and another for the lorries and trucks. Also, a four-bedroom flat was to be built to accommodate employees even though the plan was to recruit locally. The souk place was very busy with a lot of hustle and bustle.

At the end of his three days' visit he wrote a lengthy assessment report which gave the green light for the project to go ahead. Also, for reasons unknown to him, he liked the place and could imagine himself making Hasahisa his new home. He could build a house with a big garden near the Blue Nile to satisfy the Artimoga in him.

On his return to Khartoum, work immediately started on the project. Engineers, architects, financiers, and others had back-to-back meetings, and the physical construction was soon to be started. It was estimated that the store would be functional in a year's time. In the meantime, Osman made multiple trips to Hasahisa to follow the progress of the project, holding interviews to recruit bookkeepers, drivers, manual workers, security guards and others. He also travelled to neighbouring villages to decide the merchandise needed.

During one of his trips, he came to know that a nice house by the riverbank was for sale. He went to view it. It was a three-bedroom farmhouse with a huge field extending down to the river. He decided there and then to buy it. Although he had managed to save some money, the price was beyond him. He would speak to the big boss to see if the company could help, or even get a loan from the bank. By hook or crock he was determined to get that house. He informed the owner that he was interested and would revisit the following week.

The boss agreed to help him with the house. He agreed to give him an interest free loan to be paid over five years. He told Osman that this had never been done before, it was only because Osman had done exceptionally well, and he was very pleased with him. Osman was very grateful and promised the boss to work even harder. He also knew that to repay the loan he had to tighten his belt. Oh! Would this affect the plans for his wedding? What wedding? He asked himself. This just popped up from nowhere. It must have been festering, for some time, at the back of his subconscious self and came to the surface just now. It had to be the result of a cumulative effect of his mother asking him when was he going to get married. But again, the time was relevant. He was buying a big house, had a good and stable job, had his mother to please, so it was the right time to get married and start a family. He very quickly dismissed the idea, "Not now. I have a lot on my plate at the moment. First, I need to see this project through and make sure it stands on its feet," he mumbled to himself.

The physical structure was now complete, adding a beauty spot to the city façade. Recruitment was finished; all the staff had been headhunted and hand-picked from other companies in the city. They were enticed to join by giving them offers they could not refuse. Those companies were not happy, but they understood the game. Furniture was in place, shelves were stacked to the ceiling with merchandise, vans, lorries and trucks were parked and ready. There was a buzz and an infectious excitement around the place. Osman gathered all the employees for a welcome and inauguration speech.

"We should all be proud that we are part of this business. We should be working as a family looking after the business, but most importantly looking after each other. The business belongs to all of us and that should give us a sense of ownership. With honesty, hard work and dedication from your side, and good management and fairness from our side, we can go places. I wish you all the best. Oh, unfortunately the CEO is in hospital and couldn't be with us today, but he promised to drop by at the earliest opportunity. We wish him a speedy recovery."

Business was good from day one with orders pouring in from most of the villages and towns around Hasahisa and beyond. New merchandises were added to the list; more vans and van drivers were recruited. Headquarters in Khartoum were happy with the performance of the store and gave a bonus to employees. The news of this bonus, an unusual practice here, spread like wildfire all over the city, and now Osman's company became the preferred employer in the Hasahisa region. Things were going great, and everyone was happy and, business was booming.

⸻◈⸻

Chapter 7

THE NEW HOME

Osman moved into his new house by the river. He could smell Artimoga from his deck chair at the edge of the water. He was all alone in this big, beautiful house. That didn't feel right. He decided it was high time for him to get married, sometime towards the end of the year inshallah. He had no idea who the bride was going to be but would start looking in earnest. He was sure of one thing; she was not going to be from Artimoga. Life here was totally different and girls from Artimoga would not be able to cope. Most of them were uneducated and their knowledge of the outside world was very limited. Not that Osman had higher education, but having lived there for almost three years, he considered himself as a city dude.

He felt Artimoga sick and missed his family and everyone there. But he wouldn't dare go there now as the family would apply huge pressure on him to marry his cousin. That was the cultural dictate and he would find it difficult not to comply. Instead, he was going to invite his parents to come and stay with him for a week or two. They could then discuss marriage and other issues away from the influence of the rest of the family and other Artimogans. He had to think of a strategy of breaking the news that he was not going to marry his cousin. They were not going to be expecting such news. His mother would try all the motherly magic to convince him otherwise. His father would play the usual card of "what will our people say? They will boycott us for allowing you to marry outside the family. There only one case of marriage outside the family in the history of Artimoga and, that family is still suffering. May be in fifty years things will change, but till then we have to toe the line. And tell me, who is going to marry our girls if you boys marry from outside? Ah tell me." But alas! Osman had decided not to marry his cousin, and that was final. Diabetes was *rife in the family with most of his uncles and aunts affected, and some children were mentally handicapped. Marrying someone outside the family would make this less likely. This might not convince his parents and the villagers, but Osman was determined to work hard to organize a campaign to try and push back the frontiers of this outdated and harmful practice. It might take time but as the saying goes "a walk of hundred miles starts with one step." As a starting point he thought of bringing young men from Artimoga and help them start small businesses or work with him in the company. This way they would be exposed to new culture and, new ideas and, a new environment, which would help them look at life in general and, at the problem of intramarriage in particular, from a different perspective. Obviously, he would have to go slow on this as it was impossible to change such a deep-rooted practice overnight. He had to begin with himself to set an example. Now it might not be a good example in the eyes of Artimogans, but later when they looked back, they will say, "it is Osman who changed our lives for the better." It was a big responsibility and a difficult task, and a lot of people might have shied away from it, but Osman was determined to face it head on. Was he going to lose his family over this? Would he have enough support from the younger generations? Would he be considered as an outcast? Would he ever regret getting into this? He felt as if his head was going to explode.*

His parents would be there in a couple of weeks. He had to present a convincing and, a well-rehearsed argument and, must choose the right moment. There was no right moment. He was expecting the worst.

⊷⊷⊱⟨⟩⊰⊶⊶

Chapter 8

THE GIRL

*I*t was a Thursday and Osman was invited to a wedding party. *Usually, these wedding parties were held on Thursdays as it was the weekend. Friday was the only day off. One day off a week was definitely not enough. In that one day, one needed to rest from a gruelling week of hard work, do a bit of shopping, prepare for Friday prayers, visit relatives and friends. Some preferred just to chill and get away from it all. Having lived all his life on the Nile banks, Osman loved fishing. Many a time on Fridays, he would take his fishing gear and go upstream to fish for the Nile Tilapia which also bore the exotic name of Oreochromis Niloticus, and was locally called Bulti. It was his favourite fish, and he enjoyed cooking it. He always told his friends "It is easy to cook this fish. Scrape the scales off, remove the internal organs, marinate with salt, pepper, lemon, garlic, chillis, add some basil and then fry whole in olive oil," but he knew it was not as simple as it sounded. Osman also enjoyed eating this delicious Bulti fish as it didn't have those annoying small spines which might get stuck in your throat and send you flying to the hospital. He liked it served hot with a side dish of green salad, lots of onions and green chillies. Living so close to the Blue Nile, two things he must teach his children: swimming and fishing. This thought reminded him of marriage and the fact that it was time for him to go to the wedding party.*

The venue was an open-air theatre (if I can call it that) where the ground was prepared in such a way to reduce dust. This was done by covering most of the area with wet sand and then pressing it down by a steam roller. The space was divided into a male and a female seating area. The seats were arranged in a crescent shape. Between them, and to one side, was where the singers would be performing. Immediately to the left was a stage decorated with palm tree branches and assortment of flowers. This was where the bride and groom would be seated throughout the fiesta. In the male section, elders and dignitaries would be occupying the front rows, whereas in the female section the older and married women would be relegated to the back rows, while the young and unmarried girls would sit in the front rows.

The girls would be in their glamour for everyone to see. Some hearts would flutter, some would miss a beat, and some would fall in love at first sight. In addition to being seated in the front rows, girls would also perform solo traditional dances and eligible young men would approach them showing their appreciation, and get a chance to have a closer look. Wedding parties were the only place that boys and girls came that close to each other without objection from the elders or anyone else for that matter. The first step of getting married sometimes started here. One saw a girl, liked her, asked who she was, told his family, the family paid a casual visit to the girl's family, gathered information about the girl and her family, if the vetting was satisfactory and everything else was equal then the boy and girl would be officially engaged. During all this activity the girl took a back seat as if this matter didn't concern her in the least as she knew that the final decision in these matters rested with the respective families. There was a strong belief here in love after marriage. Initially the boy and girl would meet over a meal in his or her family's house. They would never be left alone. After a while they would be allowed to go to the park, but even then, a child guard would accompany them. You guessed it; the child would be given some money and asked to go and buy some sweets for himself and play with some kids nearby. The engagement period was for the boy and the girl to get used to each other, and to find out each other's likes and dislikes, or at least some of them. The wedding arrangements were usually taken care of by the families. The wedding date was decided according to star signs, but it had to be on a Thursday, that is the Thursday nearest to the chosen day.

Being classified as a dignitary, Osman was sitting at one end of the front row. This was a vantage point as the two crescents almost met there to form a full circle. From here he would have a good view of the girls sitting on that side of the crescent. Unfortunately, it had the disadvantage of being the furthest point from the other end.

The arrival of the bride and groom was announced by a loud and prolonged ululation emanating from the women's throats. The ululation was so loud it could easily be considered as noise pollution. It reminded him of those red bird males having a vocal fight over disputed territory. The couple sat on their decorated stage. The bride was dressed in a snow-white wedding dress. There was an intricate handywork of henna decorations on the front and back of her hands, extending to the middle of the forearm. The groom was in the traditional white Jalabia and a white head turban. The palms of his hands and the knuckles of his fingers were stained with black Henna. Both bride and groom appeared nervous but managed to smile at their guests. They never once looked at each other but held hands occasionally. It was well into Autumn now, but the sky was clear and starry and there was a nice cool breeze, the weather had no intention of spoiling this happy occasion.

The music band started fine tuning its instruments and the decibel from the crowd was fast reducing in anticipation. The band members were looking around from time to time as if waiting for a signal to start performing. There was a buzz of excitement whirling around the place. Osman felt a strange and an overwhelming feeling diving deep into his soul and inner self. He had never felt like this before and could not find any immediate explanation. It could just be one of those things, or was it? He started chatting with his friend, Abdulhameed, who was sitting to his right, to divert his attention from that strange feeling. That friend was the company senior accountant. They were chatting about business when suddenly, there was an explosion of music, the party had started in earnest. For a few minutes, all stayed in their chairs but then a group of friends extricated the groom from his seat and took him all round the circle receiving congratulations from the crowd amongst loud ululation from the women. Now girls were dancing individually on the dance floor, being encouraged by other girls and also by men coming close to them and raising their right arm as a kind of appreciation.

"Is next Saturday's meeting still on?"

There was no answer from Osman.

"Is next Saturday's meeting still on, Osman?" Abdulhameed repeated the question in a louder voice but still Osman said nothing. Abdulhameed shock Osman by the shoulder.

"What?"

"What is wrong with you? I asked you a question twice."

"Oh, sorry my friend. Who is that girl?"

"Which one?"

"That one in the green Toub."

"There are two girls in green Toubs"

"The taller one."

"Why are you asking, did you like her?"

"Yes."

"She is my sister."

"Oh, really?" Osman was not expecting that answer. He didn't know what to say. All this time he hadn't taken his eyes off the girl.

"You have a very beautiful sister. What is her name?"

"Samia."

"Is she spoken for?"

"As far as I know, no."

Osman gave a big sigh of relief. He had to act now. Beautiful girls don't stay single for long. That strange and overwhelming feeling came over him again, but this time a lot stronger and deeper, reaching down to the core of his soul. This was the girl for him, period. Samia, what a nice name.

"Abdul Hameed, my parents are coming in a couple of weeks. We would like to come to your place and ask for Samia's hand. Please consider this as official. I know this sounds crazy, but I am serious." Abdul Hameed nodded, but said nothing, still couldn't believe what he had just heard.

"Somehow, let Samia know as well. If they ask questions about me then, please give your honest opinion. Remember, I am serious."

"I will, I promise. Will try to tell Samia tonight. So, is Saturday meeting still on?"

"Do that please. See you on Saturday. I need to go home now."

"What about the meeting?"

"Bye."

Abdul Hameed felt that Osman was in a trance-like state, he was not really listening to him. Can love at first sight hit you like a thunderbolt? Is it that powerful to control your senses to the extent that you lose it completely? Is love at first sight common? Abdul Hameed hoped that it would not happen to him. He didn't want to be a knee jerker like Osman tonight. How could you decide to a marry a girl when you knew absolutely nothing about her. How crazy was that! What is the divorce rate of these love at first sight marriages. Abdulhameed decided to enjoy the rest of the party, but his brain was still bewildered. May be this is what people call destiny. You might not be aware, but it has already been decided by God whom you are going to marry, how many children you are going to have and when you are going to die. He was going to tell Samia about Osman tomorrow, she would not be able to sleep if he told her tonight. *"I know my sister,"* he whispered to himself, *"she is going to be a good wife to Osman, and likewise Osman will be a good husband to her."*

Abdul Hameed was sitting in the sala drinking tea after a late breakfast trying to make sure what happened last night at the party was not just a dream. He could clearly recall every word and every moment.

"Where is Mum?"

"She went round to the neighbours."

"And father?"

"He went to the souq to buy some meat and stuff."

"Come and sit down. I need to talk to you."

Samia came and sat next to him with a look of surprise on her face. Abdulhameed had never spoken to her in such a serious tone. That usual smile of his was not adorning his face this time. His body language was not reassuring, it seemed as if he was trying to choose his words carefully.

"A friend of mine, called Osman, saw you in the party last night and he wants to marry you." Abdulhameed said bluntly, without looking Samia in the face. There was a long silence before Samia cleared her throat and coughed nervously.

"Did you say he is your friend?"

"Yes, and a close friend. He is a good man; he is the manager of one of the companies here. His parents are coming in two weeks' time, and he is planning to bring them around to meet us. He is originally from the Northern Province."

"Hmm ......"

"I know you were not expecting this. You need to go and think about it."

"There isn't a lot to think about. I don't know this guy, but I trust your opinion about him. I think we have to wait and see what happens when his parents come and meet us."

Abdulhameed felt that Samia, provisionally had no objection, but is he sure enough to convey this to Osman when he meets him tomorrow.

"I agree. Can I say congratulations?"

"I don't know," she said with a grin and left the room tripping onto some furniture. She lay down on her bed and gazed purposelessly at the ceiling. What is this man like, is he tall? Samia didn't like short men as she was tall herself. She always joked, "I don't want to look down on men." Is he the man of her dreams? She started to paint a picture of him in her imagination. Tall, broad shouldered, handsome and with Afro-Arabian complexion. She imagined herself living in a big house surrounded by lots and lots of children. The voice of her father calling, woke her up from the daydreaming. She shot out of the room to the sala where he was standing with the shopping bags in his right hand.

"This is the meat and some vegetables, but I couldn't find the fresh Okra. Today we have to settle for dry Okra powder for lunch. Where is your mum?"

"OK baba, thank you. Mum went to the neighbours'; she will be back soon."

"I am going to get ready for Friday prayers. Tell Abdulhameed to get ready too."

"What is the matter with you today? You somehow seem nervous."

"No baba, nothing. I am just tired. We came late from the wedding party last night. The bride is our cousin so we couldn't leave early."

"Parties should finish early."

"I agree." She didn't agree with him but didn't want to get into an argument. She quickly retreated into the kitchen and started the process of preparing Friday lunch.

Chapter 9

THE NEWS

Friday lunch is the most important meal of the week. All the family members had to be there. Abdulhameed and his two brothers, Samia, and her parents and uncle; this uncle and her father were twins. It was considered as a weekly family meeting where issues could be discussed and sorted in a nearly democratic manner. The father, of course had the veto or the final say although he didn't use that often. These lunch meetings also strengthened family ties and brought mutual understanding and transparency. In case any of the extended family members was getting married, then a bigger Friday lunch meeting would be arranged. Two other uncles and their two elder sons, and the grandfather were also invited. The grandfather's presence was somewhat honorary as he could hardly hear anything, and his memory was rapidly fading. For him the lunch meeting was considered as a day out, and to convince the family that he could still be out and about. But his presence was important as he was the oldest in the family and this carried a lot of weight.

The Friday lunch meeting of that day was a routine one, but Samia didn't look at it that way. Last night's wedding party would definitely have its share of discussion and Abdulhameed might just drop the bombshell, also she wouldn't be able to behave normally, and her body language might give her secret away. She wanted to keep this secret as long as possible to enjoy it all by herself, before it became common knowledge. Part of her wanted everyone to know her secret and share her happiness. She herself wouldn't be able to keep it from her friends for long. Samia suddenly realized that this thing was only a few hours old, and only God knew which direction it was going to go. She had to keep it under wraps until the parents of this to be husband came and, met the family.

They all sat at the table and started enjoying her mother's cooking. It was delicious, and as usual, finger licking good.

"I liked the Imam's talk in the mosque today," said her father, trying to squeeze the words out through a full mouth, resulting in some lucky bits of food escaping the bite of his sharp teeth.

"What was it about?" Asked her mother.

"It was about how to choose a good wife and a good husband." Samia's heart missed a beat. Was this just a coincidence or was he laying the groundwork for the discussion to come.

"This is a very important subject. Choosing the right partner is the basis of a happy and a long-lasting marriage." He glanced at Samia and then Abdulhameed. Abdulhameed agreed by nodding his head, but Samia pretended to reach for the jug of water.

"By the way, a friend of mine wants to marry Samia. He told me yesterday during the wedding party. His parents are coming in two weeks from the Northern province, and I guess they will pay us a visit."

There was an eerie silence, which Samia thought, lasted for ever.

"Is he from here?"

"He moved from Khartoum to Hasahisa about a year ago. He is the manager of that new wholesale company, west of the railway station. He is originally from a place called Artimoga in the Northern Province."

"And where did he see Samia?"

"In the wedding party yesterday."

"And decided to marry her, just like that?"

"Love at first sight."

"Samia, do you have anything to say?"

"No. Baba, I only know what you know, and I will leave the matter to the family."

"OK then, will leave it until we meet his parents and then do our vetting of the man and his family. Till then keep it in the family." He glanced towards Samia and her mother and added, "Women usually find it difficult to keep a secret."

"And Abdulhameed, this man is your friend, and your opinion will be valuable." Abdulhameed nodded in agreement.

That Saturday felt like any other Saturday, lorries coming in and lorries going out, shelves being emptied and shelves restocked, staff taking orders on the phone, customers coming in person to place orders or complain about one thing or another. It felt like any other Saturday but not for Osman. His mind was somewhere else, and he couldn't concentrate. He thought of taking the day off, but it was the first day of the week and a lot of things happened on the first day of the week and he had to be present. These damn back-to-back meetings would finish only by lunch time. They were scheduled a long time ago, and couldn't be cancelled or postponed.

Did Abdulhameed say anything to his family or to Samia? And if he did, what was the response? Was there any chance that he might be rejected? Usually, a cousin would be given priority if he was interested. Osman hoped that Samia had no cousins at all, close or distant for that matter. His parents were coming soon and that was another hurdle to overcome. The meetings proceeded smoothly, but others must have noticed that Osman was not his usual self today.

"Could you please ask Abdulhameed, from accounts, to come and see me at ten past one?"

"That is in ten minutes, Sir."

"I know. Just do it." Osman said this with some impatience that the secretary was not used to.

"Yes Sir."

Abdulhameed was ushered into the office where he found Osman standing in the middle of the office. He looked tired and dehydrated with an expectant look in his eyes.

"OK?"

"OK, what?"

"About what we discussed in the party on Thursday, did you tell Samia or your family?"

"Yes, we had a discussion, all the family, including Samia, and the decision was to wait until we meet your parents and then take it from there. In the meantime, things should be put on the back burner and should be kept between us as if nothing has happened."

Osman said nothing but continued to stare at Abdulhameed, as if expecting him to add more information.

"Is that all, I need to go and have my lunch."

"Yes, that is all. Thank you. Listen, I am going to have lunch in that new restaurant near the municipality, would you like to join me?"

"How can I refuse an offer like this? I am really hungry."

"Let us go then, am also hungry." Osman was not really hungry, but he wanted to spend more time with Abdulhameed to see if he could extract more information from him. He also felt comfortable sitting with somebody who shared his DNA with Samia. He would have liked to go and meet Samia's father, and have a chat, but he knew that custom demanded his parents had to go first. He also would have liked to meet Samia, might be with Abdulhameed, but again he knew that this was not allowed and it was non-negotiable. It would only be allowed when they were officially engaged. Although Osman had decided to go ahead with this, he still needed to convince his parents and have them on his side. What if they refused to meet Samia's family? Will that be the end? Samia's family might not agree to let their daughter go to a fractured family, and Samia would not be able to go against the decision of her family.

Osman had an idea, to go to Khartoum and tell his uncle who was really open minded when it came to these matters. He could ask him to come to Hasahisa, when his parents were here and have a chat.

He drove to Khartoum on the eve of his parents' arrival. He arrived at his uncle's house just before sunset.

"It has been a long time."

"I know. I have been very busy setting up the company, but Alhamdulillah everything is fine now, and business is good."

"You did very well, and I am very happy for you."

"I am indebted to you; you have helped me a lot and I intend to repay you in some way or the other."

"Come on, you are my nephew, and this is what family is about.

"*My parents are coming tomorrow at eleven in the morning. I will meet them at the railway station and take them to Hasahisa.*"

"*I think they should come here first.*"

"*Tomorrow is a working day and I need to go back to Hasahisa to take care of a very important business there. I am inviting you and the family to come and spend the coming weekend with me in Hasahisa.*"

"*OK, that is fine.*"

"*I need to talk to you about a very important issue and I need your advice. I am planning to marry a girl from Hasahisa and as you know that might not, please my parents.*"

"*Personally, I think your parents should support you, as long as the girl is good and comes from a respected family.*"

"*I wanted you to know that I am hell bent on marrying this girl, and at the same time I don't want to create a war in the family.*"

"*Although the family's say does count, it is your life, and you have to take the responsibility for your decision. Previous experiences show that, even if there was initial objection, the family usually drops that objection just before or after the marriage has already taken place or at least pretend to.*"

"*Oh, look at you, my God, you have grown. Now it is even more difficult to differentiate between you two. Are you still playing tricks on your father?*" Osman addressed the twins, who had entered the room. The twins, laughed, asked their father if they could go to the neighbours' and left.

"*We will see what happens. Enough for now, will discuss this when you come next weekend Inshallah.*"

After dinner, Osman excused himself, and went to bed. He had a long day ahead. He needed to wake up early in the morning to go to the city centre, and buy some presents for them. He also had plans to pop into the company headquarters for around one hour, to discuss some important business.

Chapter 10

THE DISCUSSION

He arrived at the railway station, at ten minutes to eleven, where the notice board said the train was arriving on time. It wasn't long before the train pulled into the station where it terminated. Its steam engine sounded tired and running out of steam, the carriages and passengers were covered in a layer of fine dust. There was a large crowd on the platform waiting for the train, most of them in their white Jalabia and head dress. The passengers started alighting, tired and fed up with the long journey, but at the same time happy that it was all over and managed to paint a pale smile on their faces. Osman saw his parents coming out of a carriage at the rear of the train, and dashed to meet them pushing his way through the crowd. They seemed confused and perplexed with a tinge of fear in their eyes. They must have been intimidated by this large crowd. Back in Artimoga, there weren't such large crowds, and they knew everybody there, while here there was a large crowd, and they knew nobody. Add to this was the huge size of the place and the noise.

"Dad, Mum," Osman shouted when he was reasonably close to them. They didn't hear him as there was a lot of noise around, and they were busy trying to carry their luggage, and they seemed to be arguing about something. They saw Osman only when he was a few feet away. His mother dropped what she was carrying and, fell into his arms. She started crying, hugging, and kissing him and thanking God that he was well. He hugged his father and exchanged greetings.

"You have lost weight, my son, aren't you eating well? I think you need a woman to look after you."

"How are you and how is everybody there?"

"They are all well and send their regards to you. They miss you a lot. It has been a very long time."

Osman and his father carried the luggage (two tin suitcases and two carton boxes) and started to make their way towards the exit.

"We are going to go to Hasahisa straight from here."

"Aren't we going to your uncle first?"

"No. He is working now, and I need to go back. He will come to Hasahisa this weekend."

"That means tomorrow."

"Yes, he will sleep over on Thursday and Friday, and go back to Khartoum early in the morning on Saturday."

"Inshallah. I hope the bus is not going to take long because we are very tired." His father was hinting that, it might be better to spend the night in Khartoum to rest from the long train journey. Osman understood what his father was aiming at. By then, they had reached the car park and Osman led the way to his car. Osman opened the boot and started loading the luggage. His father, wide mouthed and with all the astonishment in the world on his face, stood there not believing what was happening in front of him. His mother covered her mouth with her hand in disbelief.

"Is this your own car?"

"Yes."

"You never told us you bought a car."

"Just bought it about two months ago."

"And you know how to drive it?" his mother asked not believing that Osman could drive a car. In her eyes, Osman was still that Artimogan young man who knew nothing other than looking after the farm and domestic animals. Nobody in Artimoga had a car and nobody was planning to own a car, and nobody needed a car, they had their donkeys to take them from A to B.

"Yes, of course, I know how to drive it. Had some driving lessons, then passed a driving test to get a license to drive."

Osman opened the door for his parents to get in, which they did reluctantly and with much apprehension. Osman then got behind the steering wheel and started the car with his parents watching his every move. *For the first few minutes there was a complete silence apart from his mother whispering a prayer. Most probably she was asking God to deliver them safely to Hasahisa.*

His parents were now looking in all directions, so as not to miss any of the strange sights. Tall buildings, smooth asphalt covered streets, hundreds and hundreds of cars and buses, a lot of people, but strangely, not a single donkey in sight. They noticed that people walked really fast compared to the sedate, slow tempo of life back in Artimoga. The scenery changed dramatically when they were driving on the highway. Now there were fields on either side of the highway with some haphazardly scattered villages. There were cows and sheep, happily grazing on the green grass on either side of the road, with the odd stray dog waiting for the opportunity to snatch a newly born calf. The cows and sheep come dangerously close to the edge of the road and sometimes had the courage and stupidity to cross the road with fatal consequences. Bony skeletons, on the roadside, stripped clean by vultures and wild dogs were a grim reminder. There were some roadside cafes which served meals, tea, and coffee, but Osman didn't stop at any of them as the drive was only around one and a half hours, and their level of hygiene was poor. Osman had arranged for a chef to come to his house and cook some food which would be ready when his parents arrived.

During the journey, his parents told him about all that had happened in Artimoga in the last two to three months. About those who got married, who died, who had been taken to Karima Hospital, who gave birth, boys who were circumcised, and those who contracted chicken pox, the prospect for the harvest season, the water level in the Nile and the probability of a flooding, sand dunes laying siege to the village and slowly and steadily advancing, the opening of a new corner shop on the western part of the village, the election of a new president for the village cooperative, the lorry that had broken down. They even told him about the death of the neighbour's donkey, which everybody thought had been bitten by a snake. Now everyone was looking for the alleged snake which was nowhere to be found.

"These are the outskirts of Hasahisa."

"Oh!" His parents didn't seem to be impressed, as all they could see was what looked like a shanty town.

"These are the houses of seasonal workers who come during cotton harvest season, but it is turning into a permanent residence for them. We will reach Hasahisa proper in ten minutes."

The highway closely followed the bank of the Blue Nile for a good two kilometres, and after that they parted company. At this point, Osman took a left turn, drove for a short time and then parked his car in front of a big, beautiful, detached house.

"Is there anything wrong with the car?" exclaimed his father.

"No, the car is fine. We have arrived. This is my house."

"Mashallah, mashallah!" His mother murmured in disbelief.

"Did you build it or buy it?" asked his father.

"I bought it. I took a loan from the company."

Osman saw a look of disapproval on his father's face, and he was quick to add, "It is an interest free loan and fully complies with the Islamic laws. It is halal." His father nodded his approval.

Osman led his parents into the house, his mother tripped looking at the grandiosity of the place. He took them for a tour around the house and showed them their room, and made them some fresh orange juice.

"You look tired after this long journey, and I think you need some rest. I suggest you go and have some sleep while I go and sort out a few things at work. It will take me only an hour, but it is important to do it today."

"Yes, we are really tired, and we need a long sleep. Please don't wake us up when you come back."

He brought them some prayer mats and showed them the direction of Qibla to say their prayers. They had missed the midday prayer, and they needed to do that before going to sleep. They were lucky because, the rule says, it suffices to perform only half of the prayer if you are travelling far away from your permanent residence. Islam always makes it easy for worshippers, and there are many other examples. If, for any reason, you find it extremely difficult to fast during Ramadan, then you don't have to. Instead, you can feed a poor person for each day you haven't fasted. That is the beauty of Islam.

Osman spent only one hour at work and hurriedly returned home. His parents were fast asleep and his father was snoring loudly. Osman wondered how his mother could sleep with this annoying noise. Most probably she had gotten used to it or else her hearing acuity must be deteriorating. Osman went round to the immediate neighbours and told them that his parents were here. It is in the Sudanese culture that neighbours come round to welcome newcomers or guests and usually bring them food and even gifts. This is the Sudanese for you. They are generous and welcoming people, they take good care of their neighbours, among many other nice and unique attributes.

Osman returned to his house, checked that the food was ready in the kitchen. He decided to take a nap himself and rest after an arduous day. He lay fully clothed on the sofa in the Sala and closed his eyes but couldn't really sleep. He was in a half-asleep half-awake state. He even felt that he was dreaming, but how could you dream if you are half asleep, or half-awake for that matter. While he was trying to solve this conundrum, his mother came out of the room. He sprang to his feet and walked towards her. She seemed as if she was sleep-walking, she looked confused and disoriented.

"Mother, are you alright?"

"Yes, I am fine. I am just looking for a bucket to get water for the goats."

He seated her on the sofa and literally woke her up. Dazed and confused, his mother looked around her vacantly as if saying, "Where am I?"

"Mother I am Osman. You are at my house in Hasahisa. You arrived today from Artimoga. My father is sleeping in the room. Can you hear him snoring?"

"Bismillah. Yes of course. I don't know what happened to me, it must be tiredness and exhaustion."

Osman made her a glass of fresh lemon juice with extra sugar.

"I think we should go to the hospital to get you checked up."

"No, no. I am really ok. I already feel much better after this nice lemon juice. I don't have diabetes or hypertension, and I have never been in a hospital before, so don't worry."

"Ok, go and take a shower and then we will have our dinner. The neighbours might visit later. Do you think we should wake up my father?"

"Yes please, at least to stop this horrible snoring. He never admits that he snores. You will see when he wakes up."

"Who is going to prepare the dinner?" she asked, again, with that look on her face which translates into, "where is your wife?"

"The food is already cooked; I just need to put it on the table. That is not difficult, is it?"

"Still, it is a woman's job."

"Ok mama I will get married soon, very soon in fact."

"Inshallah."

His father dragged his feet into the sala and sat on the armchair.

"I couldn't sleep at all; it must be the strange bed."

"You couldn't sleep! It is more appropriate to say that the neighbours couldn't sleep because of your very loud, horrible snoring. If it was true that you couldn't sleep then you will be the only one in the whole world who can snore while awake. What did I tell you Osman, he never admits to snoring."

"Yes dad, you have been snoring, you must have been lying the wrong way. We will be having dinner soon; do you need to have a shower or say your prayers?"

"I am hungry. I hope you have nice food for us."

"Or is this not possible for a bachelor?" his father added with a grin.

Osman felt that his parents had come with a complete plan for his marriage, he just had to sign on the dotted line. They had been passing all those cryptic messages and comments just to lay the ground for unveiling their plan. He thought of doing a pre-empted strike and tell them about his own plans after dinner. But then he decided against this. He'd better tell them tomorrow morning as the neighbours would be coming round after dinner; or should he wait for his uncle to arrive? Yes, he should wait for his uncle so it would be two against two, and that was fair play. Osman was sure that his parents would not be expecting him to marry outside the family, but will they object outright? Would they be open to negotiations and dialogue? He was sure of one thing; he was going to marry Samia.

At about 6:30 p.m., there was a knock on the door. Osman answered the door and let the neighbours in. A couple in their mid to late forties with their teenage son. They greeted his parents warmly and with such familiarity, you would think that they already knew each other for some time. Their grandparents were from a village not far away from Artimoga, and this in itself opened a wide subject for discussion. They chatted and laughed, but in the end the neighbours excused themselves and left as they noticed that Osman's parents were nodding sleepily. Artimogans go to bed very early and wake up very early too. They say you have to wake up early to get your share of God`s offerings for that day, wake up late and you miss it. Nobody knows where this saying came from, but everyone believes strongly in it. It might have a religious background. You wake up early, say your early morning (Fajar) prayer on time and you get rewarded. Obviously, there were no records to prove if that was true or not, but of course, God is great and generous at all times.

Soon after the neighbours left, his parents said their late evening prayers and went to bed. His father soon started his favourite sleeping hobby, of snoring, while his mother slept soundly through it. Osman made it a point to clear the table and keep the place in order, to avoid those intimidating comments from his parents. He made himself a cup of tea and slouched on the couch. After turning things over and over in his head, he came to a final decision for the plans tomorrow. He would tell his parents about his intentions immediately after breakfast. Leaving them, might be in shock, he would go to the bus station to fetch his uncle. On the way home, he would update his uncle, and both of them would hatch a plan or a road map of how to manage the situation.

Osman woke up with a stiff neck because of sleeping on the couch, and a cup of cold tea on the table beside him. He could hear his parents chatting in their room. Most probably they were discussing his case. He had this overwhelming urge to eavesdrop, and listen to what they were saying, but he knew too well that it is haram to do so, as clearly stated in the holy Quran. After laying the table for breakfast, he knocked gently on their door.

"Good morning. Breakfast is ready."

His parents came out of their room and sat at the table. The table was laden with choices. There was freshly minted lemon juice, yogurt, fried eggs, foul, and an assortment of fruits, along with a thermos flask, full of freshly brewed tea.

"Did you do all this yourself?" his mother asked.

"Yes, I did."

"Well done, but a woman can do it better because this is a woman's job."

"I think you should be getting married," his father added without looking at him.

"I agree. In fact, I will be getting married very soon. I was planning to tell you about it, but I thought to wait until you come here, so we can discuss it face to face. I have seen this girl, a sister of a friend of mine at work, whom I intend to marry. May be, in a couple of days, we can go and meet her family."

There was an eerie silence, you could hear a pin drop. His mother shifted uncomfortably in her chair, and his father coughed nervously, and cleared his throat, but said nothing. His parents looked at each other vacantly, as if saying to each other, "Is what we just heard, true?"

"Your mother and I will discuss it."

"Ok, that's fine. I am going now to get my uncle from the bus stop. The bus is arriving in thirty minutes. Do you need anything?"

"No," his parents answered at the same time. Osman left the house feeling a heavy burden had been lifted off his shoulders. The first step of his plan had been done and dusted. His next move depended on his parents' response. In any case he was going ahead with his plans, but

it would be nice to have his parents on board, to appear as a united front. Samia's family would have some reservations and wouldn't like their daughter to be part of a feuding family, and their grandchildren raised in an unhealthy family environment. Osman might have been considering the worst scenario, that his parents would not agree to him marrying outside the family on the basis of his Artimogal cultural background. Going with the law of probability, there was a chance that his parents would unconditionally agree to the marriage and bless it.

The bus arrived right on time, his uncle disembarked through the rear door carrying a small handbag, and a carry bag full to the brim with fruits and other stuff.

"Alsalamualaikum, how was your trip?"

"Walaikum alsalam. It wasn't bad at all."

"Let me carry this bag for you. My God, it is heavy. What is in it?"

"Some fruits and gifts for my brother and sister-in-law." It is in the Sudanese culture, that when you are visiting guests, you shouldn't go there empty handed. Not only that, you should also give them something when they leave. This puts a lot of strain on your budget, if you happen to have many such guests to visit. I expect such practices to disappear soon, as it will soon become unaffordable.

"The car is parked over there." Osman put the bags in the boot, opened the door for his uncle and then sat behind the wheel.

"I just told my parents that I have decided to marry this girl from Hasahisa. I am sure they are discussing this as we speak. I don't know what their reaction would be, but of course they might not give their blessings."

"Well, you might be right, but they might also say yes. You must give them some space. What you are going to do is not yet acceptable in Artimogan culture although I agree it has to change."

"I agree with you it has to change for more reasons than one. People have to take practical steps to change it. Please don't think, that I am doing this just for the sake of change. I really fell for this girl, call it fate or whatever you want to call it, I saw her only once and all I want to do now, is marry her. It is crazy."

"I believe this is your life, and the decision should be yours. Your parents love you, and want you to be happy. The last thing they want to do is to stand in the way of your happiness, but of course, they have all this cumulative culture and village politics to overcome."

"I know it is difficult for them but once the first sheep crosses the stream, the rest will follow. What shall I do if they say no?"

"Are you taking me home, or are we going to spend the rest of the day here in your car?"

"I am sorry, you know what is going through my mind. Thank you for your support."

"Don't worry, everything will be fine. There will be some resistance from them at first, and we shouldn't blame them for that. For them this is totally unexpected, and they have to go through the shock phase, the denial phase, and the reality phase. Leave the discussion to me, I am older than you and know your parents' way of thinking."

"I just want you to know that I am going to marry this girl with or without their approval. On the other hand, I don't want to lose them."

"I think you are looking at the empty half of the bottle."

"I am nervous about the whole thing and expecting the worst."

"I have this strong feeling that you will be pleasantly surprised."

"I hope you are right. I will be the happiest person on earth, if my parents, and all my family for that matter, agree to this marriage."

"Optimism is a virtue. We must hope for the best."

This was the first time his uncle had been to Hasahisa. He was taken aback by the grandiosity of the house and its proximity to the river.

"Wow, mashallah. A very nice house. I think I will be coming more often."

"Thank you, and you are welcome anytime. You must bring all the family and spend a few days." Osman paused for a bit and then added "I assume you will all be coming to the wedding."

"I must also invite that friend of yours who fixed the job for me, I am really indebted to him."

"You sound as if your wedding is next week. You should cool it down a little bit, one step at a time. The next step will start soon," his uncle said, while they entered through the gate of the perimeter fence. As soon as they were inside the house, they could hear voices coming from the room where his parents were. It sounded like a heated argument. Osman knocked gently on the door and announced that his uncle was here. The argument continued, so he knocked again and opened the door and told his parents that his uncle was here. They both dashed out of the room and warmly welcomed his uncle, hugging and shaking hands, the Sudanese way. This usually goes on for a while, repeating the physical acts and the verbal greetings over and over again.

"Sorry, we couldn't stop at your house yesterday as you would have been at work and also Osman had some work to take care of here."

"No worries. How is everyone back in Artimoga, and how was the trip, and how did you find the place so far?"

"Everyone in Artimoga is well and send their regards to you and your family. Are you planning to go there soon? The trip was long but not too bad."

"We haven't seen much of the place, Osman whizzed us from Khartoum to here and we have been locked in since," his father added jokingly.

"You need to have some rest after this long journey, and I am sure Osman will show you around. Of course, you will come and spend some time with me in Khartoum, and I will make sure you see the whole place, it is so nice, you might not want to go back to Artimoga."

"Artimoga is a paradise, and you don't look beyond paradise, do you," he said this with a lot of conviction and an air of inflated grandiosity.

"Shall we take some chairs and sit under that tree at the bottom of the garden and have some tea. It is very nice there in the shade," suggested Osman.

"Osman, can you give us a guided tour around the house?"

"I suggest we have tea first before the weather gets too hot." Osman started taking the chairs into the garden, and arranging them around

a coffee table under the tree. It was around eleven o'clock in the morning but already felt hot. The ample thick shade provided by the tree, together with the gentle cool breeze, bringing the moisture from the river, laden with the refreshing scent of grass and wildflowers, made sitting in the garden both pleasant and enjoyable. Osman felt like he was setting up a venue, for a meeting to discuss an important issue. His marriage was bound to be the main subject of discussion, if not the only subject, and it was an important issue. A brightly coloured bird, perched on the highest branch of the tree, started singing a lovely melody. Osman never saw a similar bird around here before. He was not superstitious, but for some reason, he thought it was a good sign. That really filled him with a wonderful feeling, he could hear the wedding bells ringing in his ears! He stood there and listened for a while, trying to break the code of the bird's language. He wished he was prophet Suliman, who was conversant with birds' language (as Quran verses tell us). The more he listened the more he was convinced that the bird was delivering a positive message. Such a nice, lovely and heavenly voice couldn't be anything but good news. The bird now stopped singing but remained perched on its high place, waiting for an acknowledgement to its message. When nothing came its way, it uttered a short sentence, in disappointment, and flew away. Khalas, Osman had no story to tell.

All sat around the coffee table under the tree. A thermos flask of black tea, cakes (brought last evening by the neighbours), and fresher ones brought by uncle, dates, and some homemade sweets. This was turning into a serious tea party. Thank God no one was diabetic.

"You should grow your own vegetables here, and plant some fruit trees; mangoes, oranges and butter fruit." Osman was about to comment on his father's suggestion, when his mother interjected.

"A house is not a house without a wife and children. Let us discuss his marriage first." She said this in a sharp and almost accusing tone. This was threatening to deflect the conversation away from fruit trees and vegetables.

"Will discuss that after Jumaa Prayer," his father said authoritatively. Mother started pouring the tea, and distributing the cakes, with a

submissive look on her face. No, she was not angry. Husband's word was final. Osman felt that his father and mother were not on the same page. It would be three against one. No contest.

"This tea is nice. What is it?"

"It is Alghazaltain brand. You don't have it in Artimoga?"

"No, we have a Ugandan tea, which we buy by weight from the corner shop. No tea bags, but it smells better as it is done on wood fire."

"Government is planning to grow tea and coffee in the south, where the weather is the same as in Kenya and Uganda."

"The vegetable plot should be closer to the house but not so close. You have to have a patio and a strip of grass."

"We, in Artimoga, put more emphasis on things you eat and save you money. What do you do with grass? Before I forget, you should raise some chicken and some sheep, you have the space for it."

"Here it is not Artimoga, brother. A patio and a strip of grass is important, as a seating area for guests specially in the evenings, also a playing area for children. Sheep and chicken need a lot of looking after but it is a good idea."

Osman glanced at his wristwatch and announced that it was time to get ready for the Jumaa (Friday) prayer. The preparation ritual includes having a shower, performing ablution, putting on your best attire, spraying on some perfume, and remembering not to eat onions or anything that causes halitosis. Also, remembering to take some money to donate to the mosque. Charity is one of the tickets to heaven. The mosque was not far but they had to go by car because the sun was too hot at midday. This particular mosque they were going to did not provide a prayer area for women. His mother had to stay at home. The grand mosque which was a lot further away, had a women's prayer area, but his mother was not bothered, as in Artimoga, women didn't go to the mosque for Jumaa (Friday) prayer. Wherever you pray, God accepts your prayer and rewards you. Might be, you will get extra hasanat (brownie points) if you pray in the mosque, but his mother was content with what she got, praying at home. She believed that, among other things, being good to others, respecting your elders, being kind to youngsters, not gossiping, being a good neighbour, being honest and sincere was paramount and got you more brownie points.

She continued to sit in the garden, under the tree, long after the men had left. The shade was receding, and it was becoming a lot warmer, despite the cool breeze coming from the direction of the river. It felt as if the sun had descended closer to earth. It was so bright and so hot; it made her squint, while making her way from the end of the garden to the house. She could feel the hotness of the ground beneath, through her sandals. She felt thirsty and parched although she had drunk some water not long ago. She drank a glass full of water and then slumped into one of the armchairs. She was not happy that Osman was not intending to marry her niece. She couldn't imagine that happening. Back in Artimoga everyone is expecting Osman to marry his cousin, and that goes without saying. How could he do that? Marry outside the family! What will her sister say? Will she boycott her? What will Artimogans say? She must make him change his mind; she must. She must convince her husband to be on her side. She knew her husband would not object as forcefully as she would, because this did not involve his side of the family. "If this boy marries from here, then every time there is an occasion involving the in-laws we have to come all the way from Artimoga," she said loudly to herself. "Where can we find the time and money for these obligations?" When it came to money, her husband might stop and listen. She could use this as a leverage. There was not a single justification for Osman to marry from outside Artimoga, or from outside the family for that matter. She didn't believe in this "love before marriage" nonsense. What was wrong with her niece? She was a beautiful and respectable girl from a respectable family. He didn't need to look any further. It was crazy that he wanted to marry a complete stranger, a girl who he knows nothing about. Her brother worked with him, that was all. What about her family? What tribe did they belong to? Marriage had to be intra-family, if not, it had to be intra-tribal but beyond that, one shouldn't even think about it. Is this the beginning of the end of our way of life as we know it? Is it changing for the better or for the worse? Is this change inevitable or could it be stopped and nipped in the bud?

She had been thinking about all these questions, and talking audibly to herself at times. She was here but not here. She was in Artimoga, but not in Artimoga. She didn't know if she was asleep or awake. Was all this just a dream? She spontaneously jumped to her feet when she heard the perimeter door slammed shut. God, the men had come back from the Jumaa prayer already. She hadn't said the Duhr prayer yet. She dashed to the bathroom to perform ablution and get ready for the prayer. She could hear them discussing what the Imam had been saying to them in the mosque. The subject seemed to be about the criteria for a good wife, and how to choose that wife. She couldn't hear much, as they were all talking at the same time. Men! She came out of the bathroom and went straight into her room to say the Duhr prayer. When she came out of her room, Osman was in the kitchen preparing lunch. For her this was totally unacceptable, for a man to be working in the kitchen. This was a woman's job. Such a man would lose self-respect.

She noticed that the kitchen was clean and tidy. How come when there was no woman around. Maybe he had hired a maid. The kitchen looked very different from hers back in Artimoga. There was no wood fireplace, no dry meat hung on a line, no oil lamp sitting on top of an old cupboard, no matchbox, no piece of a broken mirror stuck to the wall near the door, no vents high up near the ceiling for the hot air and smoke to escape. Instead, there were these large metal boxes which she came to know are called a fridge and a gas cooker.

"Go and sit there with the men," pushing him gently away from the chopping board. "Just show me how to heat the food and where everything is, will you?"

"Yes, mother. Let me help you though."

"No please, I don't want any help."

"Ok." He opened the fridge and took out the previously prepared curry, started the gas cooker, showed her where the plates, salt and herbs were. He warned her about the danger of the gas and asked her not to touch the controls. He took the jugs and glasses of soft drinks, and made his way out of the kitchen, under the disapproving look of his mother. He could hear her mumbling to herself. He joined his father and uncle, who were still discussing the Imam's talk. His father, being the older of the two, was doing most of the talking. It was a general discussion without any reference to his case, but Osman was sure that the discussion would have some bearing in the later discussion about his marriage. As he was not taking any part in the discussion, he returned to the kitchen to check on his mother.

"Go back there, I will call you if I need you."

"I just want to make sure that there is no problem with the gas cooker or anything else."

"You already explained everything to me, and I am not stupid."

"I love you mother," he said, putting his arms around her and kissing her on the forehead. She continued preparing the food and thinking about her niece. She could clearly remember the look on her face as if saying "Please send my regards to my future husband." What was going to become of her, if Osman married this girl from Hasahisa.

"The most important thing nowadays is for the man to choose his bride himself," his uncle was saying when Osman came into the living room.

"Yes, I agree but you can't ignore the culture and traditions. Family is very important. Parents and family have to vet the girl and her family and give advice as to their suitability. The blessings of parents is important."

"All this is understandable, but what happens if the man insists on marrying a girl whom his parents object to, and there is nothing wrong with that girl or her family."

"Hmm, they try to convince him."

"Arranged marriages have always been our way of life and it has worked very well when people hardly leave the village. Now young men go to big cities to work or to study and as a result develop a new way of thinking. History tells us that things don't stay the same forever, change is inevitable."

"And what is wrong with arranged marriages? We have all done it and lived happily thereafter. Don't fix it, if it isn't broken."

"Arranged marriages are always intra-family marriages. This has proven to increase the incidence of inherited diseases. The family of Tawfiq are all diabetic, because he is married to his cousin who is also diabetic. The children of the family that lives at the end of your road, all died around the age of ten years. I can give you more examples if you like. All these incidences have to do with intra-family marriages and the genes."

"Where is the food, we are starving," shouted his father, in an attempt to change the subject as he didn't know what genes are. He didn't want to reveal his ignorance by asking.

"You came just in time," said his mother, "Take these plates out and come back to take the bread and salad."

"Yes mother. Now you go and sit down, you have been on your feet a long time." Osman switched off the gas cooker.

"Leave the fire on for making the tea, so by the time we finish eating it will be ready."

"This is not like the wood fire, it takes no time to boil the water," Osman said laughingly.

"I bet, tea made on wood fire tastes better. I am sure you have already noticed the difference," she said triumphantly.

"Yes, you are right mother," he was not a tea drinker and didn't notice any difference whatsoever between the tea here and there, back in Artimoga. He had to be extra nice to her as he needed her vote later.

"Why don't you then set up a wood fireplace to enjoy a good cup of tea?"

"I am thinking about that; might be outside behind the kitchen with the tree as a shade."

"Only girls from Artimoga can manage a wood fireplace," she looked him right in the eye when she said that. He understood the cryptic message and felt somewhat uncomfortable.

"Now go and sit down. I will bring the rest of the stuff." Osman took the plates, the bread and salad and set the table. They ate while subjects of discussion ranged from weather, to cost of living, to politics. There were periods of silence in which Osman thought that everybody was *gathering his/her thoughts for the subject of the moment. As for him, the case was closed and he would be just a listener, a good listener, but the last word would be his. Still, he was full of trepidations, and mixed emotions.*

Tea was served but nobody commented on it being done on wood fire or gas fire. It was all in the head. Everybody seemed to have enjoyed it. Even mother didn't comment. They seemed to have liked the food though.

"Who cooked this food? Was it you?" asked his father.

"I gave the neighbours the stuff and they cooked it for me. Their women are very good cooks."

"Only Artimogan women know, that the best way to the man's heart is through his stomach. They are the best cooks and the best wives. It will be crazy to marry outside Artimoga."

"I am happy, that you are now ready to get married. You told us that you want to marry a girl from here. You know, that it is unknown for men to marry outside the family, even if the girl is from Artimoga."

"And his cousin is waiting for him," Mother interjected.

"Please don't ever interrupt me and let me finish what I am saying," father said firmly, "If you insist on marrying this girl, we will not stand in your way, but I want you to understand the consequences of your decision."

"Thank you, father. I really want to marry this girl. I know this is not what the family is used to, but I believe in fate and God's will. My happiness will not be complete without your approval."

"If you ask me, I think the man should be able to choose his bride. This is the ideal situation, and it has to start at some point in time."

"People of Artimoga have been marrying in the family for generations and nobody could find anything wrong with that," Mother trying to say, "the proof is in the pudding."

The discussion carried on and on, but basically everyone is repeating what he or she has said before.

"Osman, can you find out when we can meet this family. The visit is a preliminary and an informal one. We need to know their origin

and background," Father said with an air of authority. Osman was delighted with the way the discussion was going, and specially with the closing remark from his father. His mother seemed to be putting her foot down and would need a lot of convincing to change her mind. She really wanted him to marry her niece, and most probably she had already finalised everything with her sister. Her sister would never forgive her. He couldn't bear seeing his mother angry. Will she ever change her mind, if she didn't, he was still going ahead with his plans. She would be angry for a while but eventually come round, at least to see her grandchildren.

Everybody went to their rooms for the afternoon siesta. He could hear his parents arguing, sometimes in a loud voice, hopefully his father was trying to convince his mother. He found his uncle still awake, when he went into the room.

"I feel that everything is going to be ok. Don't worry about your mother. Mothers never compromise the happiness of their sons."

"I really hope so."

"You told me that this family is respected and well- known around here, that's what matters most to your parents. I am going to leave for Khartoum early morning tomorrow and I am sure I will hear good news from you."

"Try to have a private word with my father before you leave, if you don't mind."

"You heard what I said to him earlier, didn't you? I am certain that your father has no objection. He needs to meet the family and enquire about them. You need to have some names ready as references."

"At least four of the businessmen in the city are my customers and they will be more than happy to provide references. Would you be able to come, when we go and meet the family? I will arrange it for next weekend."

"I will make it a point to be there. Will also bring my wife and kids for a weekend break. My wife and your mother will together do the female part of the investigation and vetting."

At work, Osman told Abdulhameed, that next weekend his parents would pay them a preliminary visit for a general chat. Everyone knew, that this preliminary visit was the first station in the long journey of the marriage process. It is a very important station, as first impressions sometimes make all the difference, and usually both sides try to be at their best behaviour, without making that obviously artificial. They speak about general matters of interest, and ask telling personal questions but without being too intrusive. They try to suss each other out and tick a few boxes. The bride-to-be serves cold drinks, and tea, and cakes, but immediately goes back to the women's quarters and takes no part in the discussion. This brief appearance is meant to give the prospective in-laws a fleeting glimpse of their, may be daughter in-law. The visitors would be told, that these cakes were homemade, stressing that they were baked by the bride-to-be, even if they were purchased from the local bakery. The preliminary meeting is usually brief and sets the ball rolling. Following the meeting, the families start collecting information about each other, from as many sources as possible. They need to know, among other things, their ancestry, background, their relatives, standing in the society, wealth, or lack of it, who their daughters and sons were married to, and if they have been involved in any scandal.

"Can I suggest that you come and have evening tea with us tomorrow, and meet my father?"

"Ok that's a good idea."

Osman spent the rest of the day doing his routine daily work, but could not fully concentrate. His mind kept wandering, and sometimes daydreaming. Sometimes sitting in the garden, Samia by his side, and children happily playing at their feet; another time sitting alone, sad and gazing into nothingness beyond the river. He still had his fears and vague uncertainties. This marriage was not done until it was done.

He made some calls to four businessmen who were born and bred in Hasahisa and were respected by everybody. They all accepted to be referees, and give their opinion about Samia's family. They told him, that they knew her family very well and that he had made a good choice. He thanked them for their cooperation and support. "Another box ticked," he told himself with a wide grin.

The meeting with Samia's father was not easy. Osman had no idea how such meetings go, or if there were certain protocols to follow, a special way to sit, words to avoid saying etc... Her father, who seemed to be in his early fifties and looked fit for his age, worked in the post office, and had a small plantation, where he grew cotton, wheat, and vegetables. He was the secretary of the post office workers' union, and a committee member of a local sports club. He was well versed in politics and current affairs. The family was originally from Albarkal in Northern Sudan, but his great grandfather had moved to Hasahisa. Albarkal, with its famous mountain was the capital of the great ancient Kingdom of Kosh, which ruled over Northern Sudan, Egypt, and Palestine. It was the most powerful of its time. The common knowledge that the Pharaohs were Egyptians, is just not true. History of that era has to be rewritten. The fact of the matter is, Sudan is the cradle of civilisation.

The visit went fine. It was completely painless. It felt like the foreign secretary laying the ground, for the visit by the prime minister. The tea and cakes were very nice. They must have been made by Samia, Osman thought. "I need to watch my weight," he could hear himself saying. He had a sweet tooth and couldn't help falling prey to cakes, chocolates, Baklavas, and the like.

Samia's father walked him to the door, and Osman confirmed that his parents would visit the coming Friday at 4:30 after Asr prayer. As he walked away, Osman glanced back at the front door and imprinted an image of it in his memory, and wondered how many times he was going to walk through that door. The image included messages scripted with a piece of charcoal saying, "We came but you were not here." These messages are the equivalent to today's SMS, and they do the job. There was no easy way, then, of telling people when you were going to visit them, you just turned up, and if they were not there, you just left a message etched on the front door. Pieces of charcoal were everywhere, and there was no need to take any with you.

His uncle arrived late on Thursday evening, this time with his family. Osman's house was big enough to accommodate all seven of them. The children, especially the twins, were very excited; this being their first trip to Hasahisa. They were very impressed by Osman's big house and its huge garden. They started running around the garden, climbing the trees, and making a hell of a noise. They had been warned not to go anywhere near the river. None of them knew how to swim.

"Dad, can we come and live here," shouted one of the twins from the top of the tree.

"Yes, please, dad," added the other twin while chasing a beautiful multi-coloured butterfly.

"No, we can't. I work in Khartoum, so we have to live there."

"You can go and live in Khartoum and leave us here. You can visit us every weekend, you know."

"What about your school and your friends?"

"I am sure there are good schools here, and we can always make new friends."

Their father felt that he was losing the argument at the twins' level of thinking. He kept quiet for a bit, wondering what to say next. His stream of thought was interrupted by one of the twins shouting, thank you dad.

"Houses here are very expensive. Also, it will be difficult for me to travel every weekend."

"We can stay with Osman; he has a big house. If it is difficult for you to travel every weekend, then you can travel once a month," said the twins in one breath, as if they had been rehearsing.

"Will discuss this later," father said in a tone signalling closure of the discussion, and ordered the twins to go and rest, and have something to drink. The twins headed towards the house, but with a triumphant smile on their faces. What they did not know, that moving here was not going to happen. They were free to dream, of course, and enjoy living here as long as it lasted.

At dinner, the conversation was all about the upcoming visit. Everyone was taking part in the discussion, but mother was unusually quiet. *It dawned on her, that Osman was not going to marry her niece. She wished, that this discussion was taking place in Artimoga about her niece, then agreement about everything would be by default. Her sister didn't have the foggiest idea about what was going on and only God knew what her reaction was going to be. Here things were developing very quickly, and there was nothing in her power to stop it. She didn't have the right of veto. She was resigned to the fact, that this was God's will; don't stand in the way of God's will, as there is always something good in it. She said a silent prayer, wishing for the best of outcomes. The best outcome was her son finding happiness, and for her to live long enough to see her grandchildren. She also hoped that this would not lead to a rift in her family. There was no excuse for marrying outside Artimoga, let alone outside the family. This was considered as an insult to Artimogan girls and their families. Such an insult created deep wounds, which never healed. But the wind of change might have started blowing already. As a rule, change is inevitable and ultimately has to be accepted, painful as that might be.*

After Asr prayer, everyone was in their best attire, fit for a special occasion. Father was in an oversized, snow-white Jalabiya and a turban to match, and shoes made of leopard skin. Nowadays it is a punishable offence to sell such shoes as the leopard population is dwindling fast. You may get ten years for poaching, five years, and confiscation for selling leopard skin. These legal measures together with massive anti-poaching campaign, has helped restore leopard population to near normal.

"Would you please hurry up, you have been in front of that mirror for the last God knows how many hours," shouted father.

"I won't be long now," replied mother.

"You said that half an hour ago. Are you coming out or not?"

"They are expecting us after Asr prayer but no specific time. Please sit down and chill and don't work yourself up. We are going for a very important meeting; we must look good and be relaxed and give a good impression."

The children and their mother waved goodbye to the car as it pulled away, with Osman shouting out of the window, "don't go anywhere near the river."

Osman parked the car near the house, took out two tins of chocolate and one tin of dates and gently knocked on the front door. The door was immediately flung open by Abdul Hameed, with his father not far behind, who welcomed them with a broad smile. The men were led into the Diwan while mother was taken round to the women's quarters carrying the tins with her. These are two negotiating teams each with different points of interest to look into. Mother would have a close look at the mother-in-law and the bride-to-be and analyse every move and every word. As Samia would today be doing the house service, this part will be closely scrutinised.

Mother noticed that the house was spotlessly clean, everything in its right place and a lovely Bakhoor scent in the air. She liked what she saw. This of course didn't reflect the true situation but at least it was well done. When it came to the bride-to-be, she was beautiful, polite, elegant, and well spoken. She was in a long black dress matching her eyes, her long, black hair tied back in a ponytail reaching the middle of her back. "She is more beautiful than my niece," mother said to herself.

The women talked about different things but mainly about where they came from and the origin of their respective families. Although both families originated from Northern Sudan, and not far apart, there was no connection between them.

"All these cakes are baked by Samia. Mashallah, she is very good at cooking and baking. You must come round one day to taste her cooking," said mother-in-law triumphantly when they started having tea. Samia felt a little bit embarrassed, but proud.

"Yes, mashallah. Very nice cakes. I am sure her cooking will be as nice. She must have learnt that from her mother," Mother-in-law smiled agreeingly and added, "She is a lot better than me now."

"No mother, you are the best and I am still learning from you," Samia insisted.

Although everyone knows the purpose of this visit, yet women cannot discuss the issue directly as they have to wait for the men to agree on a road map. For some reason, I like the expression road map.

On the other side, to be father-in-law gave a history of his extended family, and his own history here in Hasahisa. Osman's father gave a similar account. After the initial pleasantries they immediately got down to serious business over a cup of tea and the nice cakes, allegedly baked by Samia.

"My son Osman has expressed the desire to be your son-in-law by marrying your daughter Samia. I believe you don't just marry the girl but also marry her family in a way. Obviously, we don't know your family well, but we liked what we have seen and heard so far. I am sure you know, as happens in these circumstances, that we will ask around about our family. Please don't take any offence as I am sure you will be doing the same thing."

"Well, thank you very much for coming all the way from Artimoga to see us. It is our pleasure to get to know you and your family. You seem like very decent people to me, and Osman is a well-known and respected man in Hasahisa. As you have mentioned, we will be doing the usual enquiries about your family but more importantly we will discuss your offer amongst our family and then we will let you know, inshallah."

"Inshallah. We should be going now and wait to hear from you."

"It is almost Maghrib prayer time. I think we should pray together before you go."

On the way back home father and uncle were upbeat about the meeting and seemed to be very happy about what they saw and heard. Father glanced at mother as if saying, come on then, give us a report from your side.

"The girl is very beautiful, elegant, well-mannered, and very pleasant. Knows when to speak and when to keep quiet. But of course, Osman has to meet her and make up his own mind. Her mother is a nice woman, her family is originally from Albarkal, but she was born here in Hasahisa. She is a distant relative of Mahgoub, who is related to us in a way so you can say she is family".

The conversation was music to Osman's ears. His mind wandered and he started thinking about the wedding day and how grand it was going to be and, in the process, he missed the turn to the house. Realizing that, he did a U-turn with wedding bells still ringing in his ears.

⸺◈⸺

Chapter 11

THE CONSEQUENCE

T
he news that Osman was going to marry a girl from Hasahisa reached Artimoga and spread all over like a wildfire. You could hardly find a group of people talking about anything else. The majority was against it, especially the older generation. They considered it a violation of the unwritten rule of not marrying outside the extended family, let alone marrying from outside Artimoga. It was unacceptable and unforgivable. However, a few of the younger generation thought that it was a good thing, but they did not dare to voice their opinion. In Artimoga, you accepted the opinion of the elders, even if you didn't agree with it.

Later than usual, a faint flickering light of a dilapidated oil lamp showed the images of men sitting in front of the village shop, frantically gesturing with their arms; their loud voices shattering the quietness of the night. Discussions in a loud voice denote a serious matter.

"So, what are we going to do? Are we going to let this marriage go ahead? If we do, there will be another one and then another one. Then who is going to marry our daughters?"

"What do you suggest?"

"We boycott Osman and his family if they insist and go ahead with it. Do you all remember when Hamid's son married a girl from Khartoum, and we all agreed to boycott his family? That was ten years ago. The boycott acted as a deterrent for all this time."

"I will not boycott anybody as it goes against the teaching of Islam."

"Of course, your two sons and two daughters are already married," he said this with a wry smile which nobody could see in the semi-darkness.

The discussion was charged and chaotic, and at times all of them were talking and nobody was listening. This discussion was going nowhere. This case would be the talk of the village for some time to come, but the wind of change was blowing. One by one, the men, still mumbling, slipped away, and were soon swallowed by the darkness of the night.

That night, the moon seemed to have come closer to earth, flooding the village with its bright light, making it almost possible to read a newspaper, well, the big font at least. It might have come closer to the village, to hear all the gossip and might be, to lighten the path for the villagers to agree on a decision, which would keep their social fabric intact. The nights of full moon are referred to as "the white nights." Most elders of Artimoga, like other Muslims, optionally fast the days of these white nights, possibly thanking God for bringing the moon so close to their village.

The sand dunes just outside Artimoga were washed clean by the silky white moonlight. They were arranged in a military formation, as if guarding the western front of the village. One huge dune seemed to be the one with most brass on its shoulders. On this dune, around ten teenage boys were sitting on its crisp cool sand. They were on their mid-term break of their secondary school. They considered themselves as the enlightened elite of the village, as progressing to secondary school level was not that common. This is not because of lack of brains, but boys were thought to be more useful helping in the farm. This is the view held by many villagers apart from the "out of the box" thinking few.

"Why is the moon always drawn as a smiley face? I can't see that smile now."

"I can see it very clearly. You have to have a bit of imagination, and if you listen carefully, you might even hear him laughing." All of them giggled.

"Who wants to marry a girl from the village? And who thinks Osman is right in his decision not to marry his cousin?"

"Change is a fact of life and marrying a girl from the village might one day be the exception. I am determined to go to university, and

become a doctor and work in the biggest hospitals in Khartoum. I need a wife who is educated, and preferably a doctor. An illiterate girl from the village would not fit in such a life."

"May be, in the future, village girls will go to university and become doctors."

"I think Osman is right. This is his life, and it is his choice."

"Would you do the same if your parents don't agree with your choice?"

"Parents always want their children to be happy. They will come round in the end. We don't know yet if Osman's parents are objecting to him marrying this girl."

"And if they do object?"

"They will come round when you have your first child and name him after your father."

"Guys, it is in our nature that we resist change, but change is inevitable. Sooner or later, it will happen."

"Yes, we know that, Mr. Philosopher, but right now, we are discussing a particular case."

"We are discussing a social issue which is going to affect us very soon. In ten years or so, we will be thinking of getting married ourselves. The same case we are discussing now might be our case then."

"May I remind you all, that in the last twenty years there has been only one case of marriage outside Artimoga, and if this one went ahead, it will be the second one. Aren't we just wasting our time on this subject?"

"It goes without saying, that the ones who married from outside Artimoga were those who left for Khartoum and lived there. Only one person before, and now it might be Osman."

"The numbers will increase. Just take the ten of us, we will go to Khartoum University (inshallah) for at least four years, and then most probably get a job in Khartoum or one of the big cities. How many of us do you think will marry a girl from Artimoga?"

"I think the main problem is, how to convince our elders about personal choice and the changing times. We should at least, discuss this issue with them."

"They won't listen to you, because they think they are always right, and we are only little boys who know nothing."

"I know, but we need to keep at it till they buckle. Things might last a long time, but they don't last forever. Change is inevitable."

"More boys and girls will be pursuing higher education and that will definitely tip the balance towards change."

Their discussion indicated that the buds of change, though still hidden in the foliage of customs and tradition, were beginning to flower in the spring of education and knowledge.

They chatted and chatted, before they realized that they had to go home, as it was time for the moon to go and lighten the sky of another village. The village was quiet, even stray dogs were asleep. By 8 p.m. everyone went to bed. The village mid-wife is kept busy as a consequence.

It soon became dark again, as the moon bid them farewell. After the departure of the moon, the sky exploded with millions of stars. Lying down on his bed and looking up at the Milky Way, one of the boys recalled the teacher telling them, that there are billions of galaxies, each one contains billions of stars. He felt so tiny, vulnerable, and insignificant. He wondered about the purpose of creating man, and if the world would have been a better place without humans. He went to sleep dreading the thought of his father waking him up early in the morning for the Fajr prayer, and dragging him to the mosque. Everyone goes to the mosque for the morning prayer. The day starts early and finishes early. He would rather enjoy a lie-in in the morning; he was on holiday for God's sake.

After completing the formalities of the official engagement of Osman to Samia, his parents arrived in Artimoga on a Thursday, to a charged and polarized atmosphere. They could feel that from the way people greeted and interacted with them. Fewer people than expected, visited them, and that was very unusual. During the Jumaa prayer, the Imam's address to the congregation was all about sticking to the culture and the customs, as they were tried and tested, and served their community well. Osman's father felt that the Imam was talking to him.

Immediately after the prayer finished, Osman's father stood up and started addressing the congregation.

"Alsalamualaikum. I would like to announce to you that my son Osman was officially engaged to a girl from Hasahisa. The girl's mother is originally from Albarkal, and she is a relative of Mahjoub. Her family is a very respected family, and we couldn't find anything untoward about them. This was his choice and I fully respect that. I know some of you might not agree with me, but we shouldn't stand in the way of our children's happiness."

There was a lot of loud mumbling, and a few people left the mosque.

"You know very well this is against our unwritten rule and we cannot accept your action. Still, you have time to rethink the matter over, and change your mind or face the consequences." Many others stood up and echoed the same sentiment. Only a handful agreed with Osman's father.

"As I told you, I will not stand in the way of my son's happiness and will respect his choice. It is his life, and he is old and wise enough to make his own decisions. I hope, you can see the sense in what I am saying. Sooner or later, change will happen. Who would have thought that our boys will go to secondary school and university, and our girls will go to school? Believe me it won't be long, before you face the same experience." There was a brief period of silence, followed by loud mumbling.

"In this case there is nothing more to say. Give us your final decision next Friday and we will tell you what we are going to do."

"That's fine, although my decision will not change, I would like you to think about what I have just said to you in a logical way and with an open mind." The mosque was now almost empty, as everybody hurried home to have lunch and enjoy the afternoon siesta, before they went to the fields. Although it was Friday, it was a seven-day working week. Osman's father dragged himself home with heavy feet and a heavy heart.

"People don't seem to be happy about the wedding, but we are going ahead with it."

"My sister forced herself to come and say hello to me, but I can see that she is unhappy by the way she talked, and from her body language. Her daughter didn't come. We gave our word to those people, and we have to honour it." She said that with some conviction.

"Yes. Further discussion will not be about them convincing us to change our mind, but about us convincing them to change their dogma. In the mosque, I made our position very clear. They wanted me to confirm it next Friday, and then they will decide what to do about it."

"What are they going to do?"

"If you remember, fifteen years ago, we boycotted Hamid when he married outside Artimoga. I did join that boycott, but that was a long time ago. Time has since moved on, and a lot of things have changed. Most probably they might boycott us."

"If I remember right, that boycott didn't last long."

"I am not worried about it."

"OK, let us have some lunch, and a little rest before I go to the farm. Try to win your sister over."

During the week, life seemed to be different for Osman's father. People were doing their best to avoid him, they didn't invite him for the village meeting, and they didn't ask for his opinion regarding a couple of problems, concerning the village water pump, despite his ample knowledge. He thought the boycott had already started, but was happy, that the sun still rose from the east, and set behind those grey mountains, the river Nile still flowed in the same direction, and the birds were singing the same morning melodies.

People continued to visit him but with different messages. Some warning him about the dire consequences, if he did go ahead with the wedding, and advising him to seriously rethink his decision. Some supported his decision wholeheartedly and promised to voice that in the next Friday meeting. Some supported his decision, but would not make that public. Rather than sway him away from his decision, all this actually made him more confident, that before long, it would be business as usual again.

Decision to boycott was not unanimous, there were cracks already. He was not worried about the Friday meeting, and would avoid getting into any argument. He would simply confirm his decision. That was it.

"Did you discuss it with your sister?"

"Yes, I did, she is not happy, of course, but she said, she is not going to make a drama out of a crisis. We must accept, that relations between us will not be the same and we have to live with that. Time is the healer."

"It is all the will of God almighty. These things were already pre-determined. In any case we have to say Alhamdulillah…thank you God."

"And it is haram to boycott a fellow Muslim for more than three days, especially a blood relative. She is my sister, and I understand why she is angry, but I will continue to behave normally towards her and at the same time try to explain."

"It is three months to the wedding and Osman is insisting that the main ceremony will be in Hasahisa. We should also hold a dinner party so that people will have the chance to come and pay what they owe us."

In Sudan, people will flock to a wedding dinner party, and after being fed, will contribute financially to help the newly wed and their families. Each contribution is recorded in a notebook which is safely kept for future reference. If you had donated five pounds to me then the least amount, I should donate to you, are five pounds, preferably more if you consider the rate of inflation and the currency depreciation. If there is a dispute, then the notebook will come out for confirmation. Helping each other on special occasions is a sign of a closely knit society. You don't feel alone in Artimoga. If you need anything, somebody will be there for you, if you are in trouble somebody will be there to the rescue. Still, you have to work hard and do your bit for yourself and for the wider community. Even children have a role. They help in the field. This is not child labour; it is learning the trade as most of them will be farmers when they enter manhood. Their elders are their role models. But soon Artimoga will be too small for the rapidly growing population. The limited arable land will not sustain the expanding families. Family planning is not an option. The best investment here is children, preferably boys. Girls don't work and don't generate income. When a girl gets married, her family receives money, Mahr, from the groom but this is usually spent on wedding preparations. Birth of a boy is always more welcome than that of a girl. If a woman gives birth to girls, then the husband usually goes and marries another woman, not knowing that it is his Y chromosome which determines the male sex of the baby. If a couple is infertile, it is always the fault of the wife. In Islam a man is allowed four wives, you know. Infertility investigation is not known and not available. A verse in holy Quran says, God creates some people infertile, some will have only boys, and some will have only girls. In whichever category, people say Alhamdulillah. Thank you, God. Nowadays, they still say Alhamdulillah, but the infertility clinic is available to those who can afford it.

The atmosphere in the mosque was tense and charged. Quiet, with loud anticipation and palpable disagreement. People gazing in each other's eyes as if saying "which side are you on?" Nobody wanted to be on the wrong side. Difficult decision. Many will sit on the fence and not be counted, like Britain in the United Nations Security Council vote on the cease fire in Gaza.

"As we agreed last Friday, we would like to hear your final decision."

"After much thinking and consultation and Istikhara prayer, I have decided to go ahead with the wedding. Change has to start somewhere. I fully accept any consequence." Osman's father then stood up and left the mosque.

Chaos followed. All were speaking at the same time, and in a loud voice. Nobody could hear or understand anything, no matter how hard they tried. The hundreds of birds on the huge tree outside the mosque and hidden by the thick branches and leaves, with their deafening squeals made more sense. One by one, they quietly and stealthily left. The noise finally died down, but the debate remained alive. All hurried home for the afternoon siesta. Groups of twos and threes could be seen squeezing underneath the retreating shades, squinting under the bright sun, and gesticulating. As to the final verdict, the jury was still out.

Osman's father, Mohamed, distributed the wedding invitation cards to all the men in the village. The card here is a verbal invitation delivered immediately after the Jumaa prayer. Mohamed is a very common name here, after all it is the commonest name in the world. Shout Mohamed and many heads would turn. Most probably Osman's first son would be called Mohamed.

It was mid-autumn, and the Nile was full to the brim. It is called Autumn, but rain hardly falls here. It is called Autumn, because it is not summer or winter. The water is dark brown in colour from the large amount of silt carried down from the Ethiopian highlands by the Blue Nile. The fish, finding it difficult to see, come to the surface making them an easy prey for the fishermen. It is this silt which keeps the land fertile. At the end of Autumn, when the Nile water retreats, Artimogans grow all sorts of vegetables on the Nile bank with a bumper harvest, thanks to this highly fertile land. Also at this time, dates, the main cash crop, are ripening and are soon harvested. Most weddings take place at this time of the year.

At the dinner party, most of Artimogans were there. There were some abstentions, but these were in the minority. All went well and preparations were already underway for the big party in Hasahisa. For those who accepted the invitation to attend the wedding celebrations in Hasahisa, the groom would pay for their transport and full board accommodation. This is usually considered as an obligation and factored in the budget. Some may insist to go at their own expense to reduce the financial burden for the groom.

⸻◈◈◈⸻

Chapter 12

THE BIG DAY

O sman visited his future in-laws many times and, now officially engaged, had the chance to sit alone with Samia and chat about different subjects. Evey time he met her; he became more convinced that he had made the right decision. They went to the movies once, but under the watchful eye of her brother. It was alright to sit alone with her in the reception room in the house but definitely not in the cinema. The society is not that liberal yet. Islamic religion stipulates that an unmarried couple shouldn't be all alone for any length of time, as Satan might lead them astray. The same applies if the couple is engaged. Being alone in the reception room with other members of the family in adjoining rooms, possibly eavesdropping, is not considered as being all alone. Confidentiality doesn't come first here. May be, they could get away with holding hands.

Osman was now all set. Holiday was arranged and handing over was well underway. He had to make sure that the company ran smoothly in his absence. He appointed an agency to deal with all the wedding preparations, the venue, singer, catering, the lot. He had already arranged for a tailormade suit.

This will be the first time in his life to wear a full suit, and what an occasion that will be. He wondered how he would look in a full suit, would he feel uncomfortable and uneasy? "Might be I will feel happy, special, and important, just like how Samia will feel in her wedding dress," he said to himself. He had to start learning how to wear a necktie or might be, one of his friends would do it for him. Just the thought of it made him feel suffocated. He had never buttoned up the top button of his shirt. He decided to do just that in the coming days, so as to get used to it. He wanted to be at his best on the big day. He kept asking his friends who got married recently, for tips and advice.

Being a village boy, Osman was still a virgin. He didn't have the foggiest idea how to handle the first night. What to say? What to do? How? When? Or does nature just take over? His friends were telling him different stories, according to their personal experiences. The conclusion was that this thing just happened, no plan and no algorithm. It was not even in the school curriculum. It had happened countless times before. There was no need to worry unduly. Osman shrugged his shoulders, as if saying, "That is ok then, somehow it will happen to me as well." "Samia must be experiencing the same dilemma," Osman thought, "Two novices will be trying to mislead each other to do the right thing, and later pretend to be experts in the subject and advise others."

Artimogans arrived. They were going to stay with Osman and his neighbours, a full board accommodation. It is by convention that neighbours are obliged to provide accommodation for the groom's guests, even if they have to move out themselves. Sustenance, though, is the responsibility of the groom. The house and contents have to be kept in good order and anything damaged or broken should be paid for. The wedding celebrations would carry on for full, three days. The first day was a women's affair. The groom's gift to his bride would be carried to her house in a car. It would consist of clothes, shoes, perfume, gold, cooking utensils, and other things. All these would be exhibited for all to see. Girls would flock to the bride's house and stay there the whole day singing and keeping the bride company. It has to be mentioned that a week or two prior to this the bride had an intensive course in wedding dances, which would be performed on the wedding day in front of a female only audience. The bride also goes through a beauty treatment to ensure that, she looks her best on the big day. This included daily whole-body massage with Dilka. Dilka is a treated dough, impregnated with a mixture of different perfumes and scented oils. In addition to this, she will endure many sessions of Dukhan. Literally this means smoke. Scented, smoking pieces of wood are put in a clay jar buried up to its neck. The bride, stark naked, sits on a straw, circular carpet with an opening in the centre for the neck of the buried jar, and covers herself with a thick woollen blanket, you can see only her head. She sits there for around one hour with the *thick hot smoke engulfing her body, making her sweat profusely. This practice is believed to tone the body and render the skin soft and silky.*

The second day is the Henna day. This is held in the groom's house. This is mainly for family and friends. It involves staining the palms and soles of the bridegroom with Henna stain. His close friends join in, by having one palm or one finger done. The staining is done by applying fresh henna paste onto the area, after preparing it with a special perfume, keeping the paste for a few hours at a time. The process is repeated twice, making the stain jet black in colour. This goes on while girls sing special songs for the occasion, and everybody has a good time. The groom is usually dressed in the traditional snow-white Jalabiya, along with a red silk ribbon holding a gold crescent to his forehead, and similar ribbons with golden jewellery around both wrists and one dangling from his neck. With the henna paste on both soles, the groom is stranded and is not allowed to leave the bed. He is usually reminded to empty his bladder before surrendering himself to the henna team. His hands are out of action too. He is doubly handicapped.

Some end the second day by having a party for all, as a rehearsal for the main wedding party on day three. Osman chose to keep the second day as a family and close friends affair. It was more enjoyable that way, and kinder on the budget. This house party carried on until the small hours of the morning. People slept only for a few hours and woke up to face a very busy day ahead.

Women had to prepare meals for all the guests who came from Artimoga, Khartoum and other places. Houses to be cleaned, children to be looked after. Men had to go to the market to buy fresh fruits and vegetables. Also, they needed to bring at least three sheep which they would slaughter themselves and prepare the meat.

Children of all ages were running amok, making a nuisance of themselves and annoying everybody, and at times breaking things. They were told not to go near the river, but they did. One of the adults had to assume the responsibility of a lifeguard at all times. The Blue Nile with its fast currents and deep waters was an ever-lurking danger. Many had fallen prey to it in the past. Osman hadn't thought about this when he had bought the house lying on the Blue Nile bank. A high fence at the bottom of the garden would be a good idea, but not now, please. More important things had to be taken care off first.

The most important thing on the third day is the Agid which literally means "tying the knot". This is usually done in the mosque, but the Imam can come and do it in the groom's home. Agid is the legal process, whereby a document is generated bearing the signature of the Imam, a representative of the groom, a representative of the bride, and two witnesses. After completing the formalities and the handshakes, two gunshots are fired in the air which are immediately followed by loud ululations from the women's quarters. Now everyone in the neighbourhood knew that Agid had been completed. This meant that Osman and Samia were now husband and wife. The crowd present at the ceremony, now rushed to congratulate Osman and his immediate family, and wished Osman a happy and prosperous married life, lots of money and lots of kids. The women crowded in the bride's house would be doing likewise, to Samia and her immediate family.

The stage had been prepared for the party in the open space next to Osman's house. Rows of chairs were arranged on either side separated by the dancing arena. On one side of the dancing arena, was a slightly elevated stage where the musical instruments, microphones and some special lights were arranged. On the other side of the dancing arena, a wooden structure draped in white satin and decorated with fresh flowers and differently coloured blinking lights, bearing two big (royal) armchairs, dominated the scene.

The whole area was well lit, making it easy to know who was who from wherever you were sitting. For girls, a wedding party is an opportunity to find the future husband. Culture and traditions restrict or even prohibit mixing of the two sexes. Girls go to a great length to look their best, hoping to lure an eligible bachelor, into the unexplained and mysterious experience of love at first sight, like what had happened to Osman. Girls take to the arena performing traditional dances. The girl stands in the middle of the arena, adjusts her Tobe to make sure she is decently covered, bares her head and removes her hair from under the Tobe and lets it flow down her back. This is by no *means letting her hair down! The dance is slow, with her back arched, arms extended and thrown back, head turning from side to side, then the girl shuffles slowly forward. She stops from time to time, to adjust her Tobe. There will be many girls dancing at the same time. Young men show their appreciation by crowding around the girls raising their arms in the air and clicking their fingers, producing a musical sound in tune with the song. The lucky one will have the Shabbal from the girl. Shabbal is when the girl shuffles towards one of the men, and throws her hair onto him or towards him. This might mean that she likes that particular man, or at least that man might think so.*

Now everyone was seated, members of the band took their places, started tuning their musical instruments. There was a buzz in the air in anticipation of the grand entrance of the newly-wed couple. Suddenly loud ululations and music broke the semi-silence. And there they came, hand-in-hand. Osman dressed in a dark blue suit, white shirt, blue necktie, and black shoes, and with a wide grin on his face, oozing happiness; Samia in a white wedding dress with wrist long sleeves, silvery crown, gold necklace, cheeks red with shyness befitting for a bride overwhelmed by the enormity of the occasion. She walked gingerly up the three steps, to the armchair with a supporting hand from her husband. As she sat down, Osman whispered something in her ear which brought a short-lived half smile. A stream of well-wishers approached the couple to offer their congratulations and support.

Now the party was in full swing, music blazing, people dancing, and everyone was having a whale of a time. Osman's friends held him shoulder high and paraded him many times around the arena to the delight of the crowd. The party continued into the small hours of the morning, but still everybody seemed to be full of energy. The next day was a Friday, so nobody had to worry about going to work.

Unknown to many, Osman had planned to spend the honeymoon in a five-star hotel in Khartoum and Samia and he were going to leave after an early breakfast. He kept the name of the hotel secret, as he was intending to put the "please don't disturb" sign on the room door most of the time. Scheduled room service was, of course allowed. He was going to drive to Khartoum himself. This was not advisable after a long day and a late night, but the road would be almost empty at that time in the morning on a Friday. His parents and all other Artimogans would take a chartered bus on Saturday, straight to Khartoum railway station, and from there travel by train to Karima and then by a lorry to Artimoga.

Samia was now at her new home, but not yet the lady of the house. She was being treated as a queen, and everybody was at her service. Osman lay on a bed with his eyes closed to catch some rest, while breakfast was being prepared. A mechanic from his company checked the road worthiness of his car, and gave it the all clear. Samias mother was double checking, that all her daughter's things had been packed, especially the perfumes and the other "stuff" related to the honeymoon.

After breakfast, suitcases were taken out, and put in the boot of the car and some on the backseat together with some small bags and cartons.

"What is all this luggage for? We are only going away for a week," exclaimed Osman.

"You will understand and appreciate when you find out," answered his mother-in-law with a wink, at the same time looking at Samia, who chose to look down at her feet with a hint of shyness and embarrassment, while everyone else giggled. Osman pretended to be looking at the front, car tyre and discussing something with the mechanic.

It was an emotional farewell. Samia and her mother were in tears hugging each other, mother whispering something in her daughter's ear and in a crackling voice, Samia could be heard saying "Yes mother, I will remember." God knows what this thing was, that she promised to remember. Osman hugged his mother and kissed her on the head. She wiped some tears with the edge of her Tobe.

Osman opened the car door for Samia and helped her into the front seat, closing the door behind her. Before he got into the car, he shouted to his father reminding him to leave the house keys with the neighbours. The car moved away slowly, everyone waving and wishing them all the best, till the car disappeared in a cloud of dust. After two minutes of a bumpy ride, they reached the main highway leading to Khartoum. Khartoum was about 150 kilometres away and normally was *a two hours' drive. It took Osman three hours, as he drove slowly and had to take many coffee breaks, to keep himself refreshed and awake.*

It was early afternoon when they checked into the hotel. The room was on the top floor and the management provided red bed sheets, a nice bunch of flowers, a box of chocolates, and a best wishes card. There were extra bath and hand towels. It was the only occupied room on that floor. It seemed the management had thought of everything, literally everything, after all it was a five-star hotel.

This was Samia's first escapade to Khartoum, but she was not expecting to see much of it as the time was short, and for another obvious reason.

Samia sat on the edge of the bed while Osman offloaded the suitcases. There was awkwardness in the air. Whatever they tried to talk about, seemed to be inappropriate. While Samia was in the bathroom, to change into a more comfortable dress, Osman prayed two Rakaas and begged Allah that he and Samia live happily together and have a happy, loving, and successful family.

They spent a lovely week in Khartoum. They hadn't seen anyone they knew, had visited nobody, they spent most of the time knowing each other. They managed to find time to visit a few places and have dinner in some of the top restaurants in town. They were not used to such luxury and if they had stayed any longer, they would have been spoiled beyond the point of redemption. But they would have soon come down to earth with a bump.

Artimogans arrived home safely to a lukewarm reception from some, and an enthusiastic upbeat welcome from others. Life carried on as before with no public discussion about the wedding. The sun still rose from beyond the other riverbank and set behind those grey mountains. Most Artimogans concluded that what was meant to be, had happened and they had to move on. Osman's cousin now felt like an outcast and only God knew how long it would take her to get over it. She was hoping that one of her other cousins from her father's side, would rescue her, but the competition was stiff from the other female relatives of her age.

Chapter 13

THE LITTLE FAMILY

*T*wo months after the wedding, Samia started to feel sick, especially in the mornings.

"You wasted no time, that is my girl."

"What do you mean mother?"

"Feeling like this in the mornings means that you are pregnant."

This produced a mixed feeling of happiness and something else which she couldn't grasp. She said nothing, but kept looking at the tears in her mother's eyes. Suddenly her body, which she knew forever, felt different, different in a different way.

"How can I make sure?"

"I am telling you that you are pregnant, take it from me. I have been pregnant seven times, so I know. You will not see your periods from now on. Of course, you need to go to the hospital and see a doctor."

"Shall I tell Osman?"

"Yes, you should." That was said with much conviction. This woman knew what she was talking about.

"Ok. I will." Samia started thinking of how she was going to break the news, and what would be Osman's reaction.

Osman came home a bit later than usual and didn't seem to be particularly happy. This had happened a few times before, and Samia in her own wisdom, never asked him what had happened. She would bring him a glass of cold, fresh orange juice and let him have a lie down for a bit.

"Shall I bring you lunch?" People usually had lunch when they came back from work around 2 p.m.

"Yes. Thank you."

They sat down to eat in the verandah which was made cool by the air conditioner, something which encourages your appetite on top of the fact that Samia was a very able cook.

"How was your day?"

"Not very good I am afraid, one of those days, but nothing to cause sleepless nights. How was yours?"

"I was feeling tired."

"Don't work hard. I know this house is big and maybe, we need a maid or somebody to help you."

"It is not overworking, which is making me feel tired."

"What is it then?"

"I just discovered that I am pregnant."

Osman's hand froze halfway in its journey to his mouth, which remained wide open and kept staring at Samia as if he had seen her for the first time. Suddenly he got up, let out a loud shriek, picked Samia up and twirled her round and round shouting, "I am going to be a father."

"Careful, careful. The baby," pleaded Samia with a happy laugh.

"Oh yes! We need to book an appointment with the top obstetrician in town."

"Would you like a boy or a girl?"

"I want a healthy baby, preferably a boy, but I don't mind a girl. By the way, how did you know you are pregnant?"

Suddenly a dark cloud of doubt hung over Samia. She didn't yet have a confirmatory test, her period might be late for any other reason, and the same was true for morning sickness. She just took her mother's opinion to be the truth. Did she speak too early?

"My period is late, and I feel sickly in the morning and my mother said I am definitely pregnant." Samia said with a little less enthusiasm.

"Well, let us do a test this evening in one of the clinics. I am sure you are pregnant; I can sense it." Osman said, holding her hand.

Now pregnancy was confirmed beyond any doubt by the test, period didn't make any appearance and Samia kept getting sicker in the mornings and with some strange food cravings. Her mother and sister were at hand to help with the housework. By the third month the morning sickness had all but disappeared, she was eating normally, and she was back to her normal self again, but developed a bit of a belly. Her mother's and sister's visits were becoming less frequent, she could manage by herself, thank you.

It was a baby boy and they called him Omer. In Sudan, naming of the baby is officially done on the seventh day after birth, and the occasion is marked by a family party where a sheep is sacrificed. Osman decided to circumcise Omer on that same day. At this age it is usually done in a hospital, but older children are circumcised at home by a non-medical person who inherits the skill from his father. It is a lucrative part-time job, considering the high birth rate and the fact that most boys are circumcised just before they start school. Although he doesn't have any medical background whatsoever, he does the job well and claims that doctors are not as good. His father and grandfather had the same belief which is shared by a lot of people, and their results speak for themselves. Having said that, if anything goes wrong with their circumcision, they take the boy to the hospital; for the doctors who are not as good, to sort out the problem.

For older children, circumcision is a happy occasion. They get new clothes for the occasion; they are the centre of attention and envy of the younger boys. They receive money and presents, from their parents, relatives and friends. They are the stars of the party, and they are spoilt rotten. Circumcision is done without anaesthesia and in full view of a large, curious audience. Although the procedure hurts, most boys do not show any sign of distress, and tears are kept in their lacrimal sac. They were told, that now they are men and men don't cry or even flinch. They feel proud and manly when they pass the test. For boys, circumcision is a milestone, the first step into manhood, and they enjoy it very much. In that way, it is unfair for baby boys to be circumcised as they miss all the enjoyment and razzmatazz that go with it. Later they might think, they were born without a foreskin. Doctors will tell you that baby circumcision is better as it has less complications and is less distressing and done in the hospital under aseptic conditions. Still, the number of circumcisions done at home, far outstrip those done in hospital, and without any major problems. People think, doctors should turn their attention to something more complicated. Before hospitals, all boys were circumcised at home, and everybody was happy with that, and this practice may continue for many years to come. Change is always difficult and not readily acceptable.

The family grew bigger and bigger, and the fifth son was named after Osman's father who had passed away three months earlier. There were also three girls. Big family is a norm in Sudan and children are considered as a good investment in the fabric of the extended family system.

Chapter 14

THE DOCTOR

O mer, the elder son, excelled at school and gained entrance to the prestigious University of Khartoum medical school. This medical school was established in the year 1924 by Sir Lee Stack, the then governor of Sudan during the British colonial era. The medical school was named after Lord Kitchner who led the military campaign which ended the rule of the Mahdia, and who died in 1916 after his submarine was torpedoed by the Germans; his body had never been found. University of Khartoum is considered to be one of the best, if not the best university in Africa. Being the only university in Sudan at that time, only the crème de la crème can gain entry. The rules are tough and high standards are maintained at all times. If you fail your exams, you are dismissed, that's it.

Omer sailed through the high waters of the medical school for six years without a problem and safely reached the bank of graduation. People started to call him "doctor" the minute he was admitted to the medical school. Now he was a real doctor, ready to serve his community, fully aware of all the challenges and hard work ahead. He always believed, that prevention is better than cure and that resources and budgets should be directed towards the control and prevention of endemic diseases and childhood diseases, rather than being spent on the clinical side. He also thought, that the management of the aftermath of natural and man-made disasters leaves a lot to be desired from organizations like the WHO and the United Nations.

Might be, he was thinking far ahead, he needed to concentrate on the job at hand. He had to do his one-year houseman-ship in a major hospital, to learn the ins and outs of medicine which would prepare him for his assignment at a single doctor hospital the following year. This is called the hardship year as it is usually spent in a remote *area with meagre facilities. You are all alone there and you have to deal with any case which comes through the door. You are the jack of all trades, but may be master of none. You are the doctor, hospital manager, responsible for signing of contracts, and looking after environmental health, and for your position in the community, a lot of people would come to you with their personal problems and family issues. The clinical part of the job, although daunting, is the easier part because at least it is in the Medical School curriculum. In contrast there is nothing in the medical school curriculum about hospital management. Doctors have to depend on common sense, and taking the advice of the hospital accountant, and the head of nursing. The doctor is unfortunate if he seeks advice from people, who would take advantage of his inexperience and vulnerability. A lot of money could be made from contracts, if there is corruption, and the novice doctor usually doesn't have the faintest idea about these contracts. These contracts are for providing meals for inpatients, supplying staff uniforms and operating theatre scrubs and footwear, and so on. It might take the doctor a couple of months, or longer, to suss things out. The position of hospital manager comes with a lot of responsibilities. This is specially compounded if the doctor is transferred to a hospital, which has been without a doctor for some time. Some doctors refuse to go to very remote hospitals, or those in conflict zones and with safety concerns, and so a hospital might be without a doctor for a few years. During these years, all hospital services deteriorate, community health programmes come to a standstill, and the local people see no point of attending a hospital without a doctor and instead, go to the next, closest hospital. Consequently, the hospital loses its importance and dynamics, and more importantly, loses its continuity of services. A doctor coming at such a time, would have a lot on his plate. The first few months of his tenure would be spent in making the hospital stand on its feet again. Infrastructure improvement, staff recruitment, training and retraining, medicines' availability, are just a part of the challenges facing the novice, inexperienced doctor.*

Omer was appointed to go to Abu Hamad Hospital. Abu Hamad is a town, sitting on the tip of the bend of the Nile, where it changes its northerly direction and turns sharply south westerly. The name literally means the father of Hamad. In Sudan, as in most Arab countries, after the birth of your first son, people start calling you by another name. If your child's name is Omer, then you are known as Abu Omer. The original name on the birth certificate remains the same though. This Abu Hamad, after whom the town of Abu Hamad was named; his first name was Rafi, and he was the grandfather of the Rifaiya tribe. His first son was called Hamad. He was buried in Abu Hamad and his tomb is still there to this day. Maybe, many people living in Abu Hamad do not know this fact of history. At the time of writing this book, Abu Hamad was devastated by floods which damaged hundreds of houses and obliterated the whole town. The fate of the tomb is not known. If the town is relocated, it is going to be called Abu Hamad. Such a disaster happens once in a lifetime, and this might explain the fact that people rebuild their houses in the same path of flowage which devastated them. This time, the losses were so big that the population of Abu Hamad is going to the higher ground. The government will encourage that, or even make it mandatory.

Dr Omer realized quite early, that preventative medicine is more important and cost effective compared to clinical medicine, and more resources should be allocated to it. Endemic diseases in Sudan are the main cause of mortality and morbidity. Treatment of these diseases is expensive, compared to the relatively inexpensive and effective preventative measures and health education. This applies to all the poor countries in the world. He would like to help them all if he can. He also realized that disaster management was lacking in Sudan, and something had to be done about it. A young enthusiastic doctor, who saw that a lot of problems needed to be solved and he wanted to take part in solving them; he liked clinical medicine very much, but felt that his heart was in preventative medicine and related humanitarian aspects. This really came home to him, when he was seconded to Alzaidab hospital. Alzaidab is a big town about 250 km south of Abu Hamad. It had a large irrigation scheme which was privately owned, it was a very successful scheme which was well run and employed a lot of local people. Unfortunately, this scheme was nationalised by the Numeri Government, and since then services deteriorated, resulting in poor canal drainage, creating spans of stagnant water. This provided ideal conditions for the breeding of mosquitoes, with a sharp increase in malaria cases. The hospital started receiving a large number of cases of cerebral malaria with high mortality, especially among children. Dr Omer, realizing the seriousness of the situation, summoned the help of preventive medicine department in the Ministry of Health. They promptly attended to the situation, and started intensive house fumigation, cleared mosquito breeding places, mass testing and treatment of the population. Within one-month, Alzaidab was declared malaria free apart from a few sporadic cases. This convinced Dr Omer, and beyond any doubt, that prevention is far better than cure.

Towards the end of his secondment to Alzaidab, came an opportunity to join a master's degree course in Community and Preventive Medicine; Dr Omer jumped on it in a flash. He did this out of interest and the firm belief, that Community and Preventive Medicine was the way forward to solve most of the health problems in Sudan. He was the only applicant and that was not surprising. This branch of medicine was not very popular as it lacked the glamour and the prestigious social status of its clinical counterpart; was not as lucrative, and in most cases, you needed to work in remote places, which involved hard, field work and a lot of time away from your family. It was a shame, that such a vital specialty was gauged on the basis of personal and worldly parameters, affecting its popularity and consequently, medical staff recruitment.

"Why did you apply for this job?" asked the interviewer.

Dr Omer hadn't prepared for the interview as he didn't know what to do in the way of preparation. This was his first job interview ever. He also kept his application secret, knowing that his family would be expecting him to take the line of clinical medicine as expected from the great majority of the medical school graduates.

"Mostly out of interest," Dr Omer replied, trying to add more but was interrupted by the other interviewer.

"And what else?"

"Preventative and Community medicine is the best way to tackle endemic diseases, as it is cheap and more effective, but this is not reflected in the government budget allocation." He told them about his experience of the malaria outbreak in Alzaidab.

"Did you know how cheap or how expensive was the cost of the preventative measures in this case you told us about?"

"No," Dr Omer said embarrassingly.

"So how could you say preventative medicine is cheaper"?

"Well, before the preventative team arrived, I used to have at least fifteen inpatients of cerebral malaria, with high mortality from multiple organ failure and coma. Half of those patients were children. One month after the arrival of the Public Health team, only a few sporadic cases were seen. I don't think you can put a price on human life. You can almost eradicate a disease by means of prevention, but you can't do that by treating clinical cases."

"I agree with you. There is another thing, you know that most of your work will be field work, and in remote areas; will this be a problem?"

"I am very aware of that."

"Are you married?"

Dr Omer was taken aback by the question. He had never thought about marriage. "Marriage? I graduated less than two years ago, for goodness' sake," he said to himself. He didn't even have a bank account yet, and no one in mind to marry.

"Not thought about that yet. I hope it is not a prerequisite for landing the job."

"No. It is not. In fact, this job might not be suitable for those who are married, and especially those with young kids. This doesn't mean that married candidates can't get the job."

"It will be a few years before I get married. Need to sort out my professional future first."

After half an hour of interviewing, Dr Omer was asked to wait outside. There were no other candidates waiting to be interviewed, which he found strange. Might be some candidates were coming another day, or some might have already been interviewed, he thought to himself. He waited for fifteen minutes, before being called in again.

"After deliberating amongst ourselves, we are very pleased to offer you this post, as we think you are a suitable candidate."

"*Thank you very much, I accept your offer.*"

"*When would you be able to start?*"

"*I need to give one month's notice to the hospital, where I am working now, and another two weeks to hand over to the new doctor, and a further two weeks to relax and rewind.*"

"*That is fine. Do you have any questions for us?*"

"*No. I read a lot about the post, and I roughly know what is involved, but if anything comes to mind, I will let you know.*"

"*Excellent. You know where to find us.*" *With this the interview panel stood up, shook hands with Dr Omer and wished him all the best.*

As Dr Omer had always believed in the importance of public health and preventative medicine, he felt a sense of relief and satisfaction about his new job and role. Preventative medicine is cost effective compared to clinical medicine, considering the limited financial resources available in Sudan at that time, and as they say, prevention is better than cure. From this early stage in his career, Dr Omer was thinking of offering his services and expertise to other countries in the third world (a misnomer), which have similar problems and challenges as Sudan. He was a strong believer in one world, one people, love and help thy neighbour, share your wealth, and knowledge with others. This might sound idealistic and difficult to achieve in our world of today, but Dr Omer believed that nothing is impossible, if you put your mind to it and persevere.

Endemic diseases like Malaria, Bilharzia, Leishmaniasis, Sleeping sickness, Onchocerciasis, Tuberculosis, Hepatitis, Typhoid; together with childhood diseases like Measles, Whooping cough, Polio, Diphtheria, form a formidable challenge to the healthcare system. This was the challenge Dr Omer was very aware of; a challenge he accepted and decided to face head on. He was determined to push back the frontiers of these endemic diseases, and to eradicate the childhood diseases through mass vaccination. That was very ambitious, you might say as people had tried hard before him with little or no effect. But again, other countries had managed to eradicate these endemic diseases and were almost free from childhood diseases, which meant that it could be done. Dr Omer was not underestimating the task in hand, but he was determined to give it all.

At this stage of his career, he needed to obtain some further qualifications in public health and spend an apprenticeship period with one of the gurus in the field of public health. Soon after joining the Public Health Department of the Ministry of Health, he was sent to Alexandria University to do a diploma in Public Health. That was in 1978. Dr Omer got married on the third of May 1978 while he was in Alexandria, and his wife Thuraiya joined him there. Later on in 1985 he was sent to Ain Shams University in Egypt to study for a master's degree, which he successfully completed in the allocated time of two years. This master's degree course was conducted and supervised by professors in the field of public health from Arab countries, who were at the time living in exile. Amongst them was professor Mustafa Khojaly from Sudan, who was a well-known figure in the field of public health, with many publications to his name, and many PhD and master's students got their degrees under his supervision. Also, with his vast experience in field work, he was considered as a reference and an authority in epidemiological work and its execution.

Dr Omer worked in Darfur province in western Sudan, for a few years. He was responsible for general public health schemes, childhood vaccination programmes, especially polio vaccination.

During that period, intelligence gathering suspected that a large quantity of contaminated sugar entered Darfur Province from Chad through the long, leaky border. As this was a public health issue, Dr Omer summoned the chief of police, chief of the army garrison, the tribal chiefs for an urgent meeting. After short deliberations, it was decided to intercept the suspected cargo before it entered the market, where it would be more difficult to trace. In Northern Darfur, and not far from the border, ten large trucks loaded with hundreds of sacks of sugar were intercepted and the cargo impounded and those onboard arrested. Dr Omer and his team took random samples from the sacks and ran some laboratory tests on them. Fortunately, no contaminants could be identified, and the cargo was released to the owners, with an apology and an explanatory note of what had happened. This had been a good exercise, and a valuable experience of different departments working together as a team, and dealing speedily and appropriately with a situation bringing it to a satisfactory conclusion.

Dr Omer was then transferred to the Blue Nile Province. Blue Nile Province is situated in the south eastern corner of the country, bordering on Ethiopia, and now South Sudan. A large number of refugees descended on it from Ethiopia, Eritrea and some were displaced from South Sudan. Refugees bring with them massive public health challenges, especially when they come to a poor country like Sudan. Help from the World Health Organization and other charitable organizations, might assisted to improve the situation.

Dr Omer, with the limited resources available, managed to look after those in the refugee camps, paying special attention to children, women and the elderly. His initiatives included children's vaccination programmes, health education in reproductive health, personal hygiene, and simple preventative procedures like hand washing after being to the toilet, and before sitting at the table for a meal, wearing long white garments to reduce mosquito bites, and others.

Dr Omer was enjoying his job in the Blue Nile province, and making a huge difference to the health of the local population, which was reflected in the lower incidence of endemic diseases, in the great reduction in the incidence of childhood diseases, and in the greater awareness of the general population, about personal hygiene and cleanliness.

It seemed, that his good reputation had travelled far and reached the capital, Khartoum. He was asked to come to Khartoum, to take the position of assistant commissioner for public health. Delighted as he was with this promotion, he was sad to leave the Blue Nile province, as there was a lot still to be done, and he would have liked to finish what he started. But again, he couldn't turn down this opportunity of promotion. He hoped, that whoever replaces him, will continue the good work he started, and realise his dream that the Blue Nile province would be free of childhood diseases, and almost free of endemic diseases.

He learnt, that a close friend of his, a classmate, would be coming to take over from him. He was very delighted with the news, as he knew that guy was a hard worker, dependable and trustworthy; and he was the one to carry on what Dr Omer started, to fruition.

The handover took around a week, and the farewell parties took another week. Dr Omer delighted with the promotion, was tinged with some sadness, as he was going to leave the many friends he had made here, and leave the place where he had so many fond memories. He stayed on for another week to relax and recuperate and get ready for his next move.

On the day of departure, he collected his things and dumped them in the boot of the Land Rover which the driver had checked for its road worthiness, the night before. Dr Omer had bid farewell to his friends the night before as he was setting off in the ungodly hours of the early morning, when the birds are just waking up and starting to chirp. The roads were empty and deserted, as it was early morning on a Friday. When the car reached the outskirts of Algadarif, Dr Omer glanced back at the city, not knowing that this would be the last time he would ever set sight on it. All along the way, he was deliberately engaging in conversation with the driver to make sure that he was awake and alert. He reached Khartoum, just after the Jumaa prayer time, and immediately went to his brother's house, where he would be staying till a house was sorted out for him, now that he was a high-ranking government official. His brother, and some relatives were waiting for him with lunch and congratulations.

Lunch was a delicious, typical, Friday lunch made of Gorrassa which is a thick wholemeal wheat pancake, floating in an abundance of dried okra and dried meat curry, with a side dish of hot, red peppers, lemon juice and white onions. This is usually followed by a dessert of some sort. Black tea is a must, before everybody goes for a long, afternoon siesta. Contrary to popular belief, black tea actually helps you to sleep, especially after a big lunch on a Friday afternoon.

After coming out of the unconscious state of the afternoon siesta, Dr Omer had a shower and performed the Asr prayer. His brother then took him to visit some elderly relatives, who for logistical and mobility reasons, couldn't visit other people themselves. It is also a sign of respect, to visit older people in their homes. On coming back home from their outing, Dr Omer and his brother discussed a lot of topics.

"This job of assistant commissioner for health is a big job, and I am surprised that you were chosen for it."

"Why are you surprised, you think I am not up to the job?"

"Not that. You see, the ruling party of these Muslim brothers will give such a job only to someone, who is affiliated with them."

"I am definitely not affiliated with them; in fact, I hate them."

"Just tread carefully and don't trust any of them. Stay away from politics and just take care of your work. Working in Khartoum in such a position is different from working in Darfur, and the Blue Nile Province. Here politics goes into everything and if you are not affiliated to these people, you are immediately at a disadvantage."

There was a long pause from Dr Omer. Now he was wondering, if this was the right move. Was he going to be happy here? Will he be forced to toe the line of these Muslim brothers, and adopt their corrupt ways? Why did they offer him this post in the first place? Should he have said no?

"I am supposed to meet the commissioner this Sunday, so let us wait and see."

"Hope all goes well. It will be nice if you stay and work in Khartoum, all things being equal, as they say."

Chapter 15

THE TURNING POINT

*T*his summons to Khartoum proved to be a turning point in Dr Omer career. It turned his career path hundred and eighty degrees. It deflected his plans into an unexpected and unchartered territory. What did happen was out of this world and completely out of the blue.

On Sunday morning Dr Omer woke up early, said his Fajr prayer, read some verses from the Quran, fixed himself a breakfast and a mug of black coffee and sat in front of the TV set, to see what is going on in the wider world, but, after a very short time, he switched it off as it was all depressing news; Israelis killing Palestinians in the West Bank, Americans bombing areas in Afghanistan killing many civilians, floods in Bangladesh and drought in Somalia, earthquakes in Iran, and receding ice cap in the Arctic. Two colourful birds perched high on the Guava tree, attracted his attention. Both were chirping loudly, and at the same time, as if they are arguing. "They must be husband and wife," he thought to himself with a wry smile. The husband must have woken up on the wrong side of the bed. He wished he could understand birds' language to know what they were arguing about. He, all of a sudden, became very curious. Prophet Solomon spoke birds' language fluently and it is unfortunate that he didn't share that knowledge with the rest of humanity, and didn't record its alphabets, and grammar and explain its acoustics. If he had done that, we could have enjoyed bird's songs more, as knowing the lyrics, augments the enjoyment.

Dr Omer left the house at about 8am. It was (surprise, surprise) a sunny day and even in the early hours of the morning, you could feel the heat, which was a sure indication that it was going to be a hotter day. He hailed a taxi, which took him through pothole infested streets to the Ministry of Health on the banks of the Blue Nile. That area of

Khartoum was very beautiful, but there was not a single hotel in sight. All the buildings were governmental buildings, and most of them were built during the British colonial era. Ideally all the areas on the Nile banks, and specially the area where the Blue Nile meets the White Nile, should be a sightseeing area with hotels, cafes, restaurants, cinemas, clubs, river boats, and what not, and teeming with tourists from the four corners of the globe.

He headed towards the junior minister of health office, and entered a big room with expensive looking armchairs, and a carpet to match. The secretary, a young beautiful girl, wearing a hijab and generous facial make up, was sitting at a huge desk with an upmarket swivel chair. She was of short stature, compensated for by wearing pointed high heels which required a lot of skill to walk on.

"Good morning, Sir. Are you Dr Omer?"

"Good morning. Yes, I am."

"His excellency is expecting you. Please take a seat. Would you like some tea or coffee? He is in a meeting, which will hopefully finish in ten minutes or so. Sorry about that."

"That is fine. Tea if you don't mind, black and no sugar, just had some coffee at home."

"We have a very nice tea, specially sent for his excellency from Sri Lanka".

"I hope the minister paid for it," Omer said to himself.

The secretary brought a cup of that special tea from Sri Lanka, and a glass of water. The tea tasted like any other tea, and Dr Omer's taste buds didn't detect anything special. He sipped the tea while stealing glances at the secretary, who was busy looking at her face in a small handheld mirror.

Two gentlemen came out of the minister's office, exchanged some words with the secretary and hurriedly left. The secretary, after checking her makeup for the umpteenth time took some files, and walked, somewhat unsteadily into the minister's office. She emerged five minutes later, and standing at the ajar door, announced, "His excellency will see you now."

Dr Omer walked past her, as she stood by the door, and a whiff of an expensive Parisian perfume filled his nasal sinuses. He had never tried expensive perfumes before, and that was an assumption on his part, as Paris is famous for nice perfumes.

The office was huge, the size of a studio flat. There was a big desk, and an even bigger portrait of General Elbashir behind it. The Minister warmly welcomed him, and guided him to a round table where two gentlemen were sitting. He introduced them as the commissioner of Khartoum and his assistant for clinical medicine.

"Welcome Dr Omer. How was your trip from Elgadarif?"

"It was fine. Thank you."

"I must commend you on the excellent job you are doing in the Blue Nile province. All the reports, which came out of there are very good."

"Thank you. Still there is a lot to be done, and as you know there is a lot of poverty, ignorance, poor infra-structure and poor development."

"Yes, I agree but as you know the government is doing its utmost to improve all that."

There was a period of uneasy silence, then the minister suddenly stood up.

"I don't know how to say this Dr Omer, but we have already filled the position you were coming for, because unfortunately, your report from the security authorities will make it very difficult for us to employ you in such a senior position. Can I suggest that you go back to the Blue Nile Province, and continue the excellent work you were doing there."

"I already handed over to someone else there, and you know that. Going back is out of question." He found all this very strange and couldn't wrap his head around it. "Anyway, thank you very much for wasting my time, and I am sure I can sort something out."

Dr Omer stood up, and left the room, slamming the door behind him. The secretary was startled by the thud, but before she could say anything, Dr Omer was out of sight in a flash. When he was out in the street, he pinched himself to make sure that this had actually happened. He walked along the pavement in a trance, as if in a dream, with everything around him seeming unreal. He sat at a café in Alneel avenue, and ordered a coffee. He gazed in the distant nothingness, and his mind wandered away taking him on its wings across vast forests, and plains and over rivers and blue lakes. He took a subconscious deep breath, and he could smell the lovely fragrance of wildflowers, and fresh air, laden with the moisture, and smell of a distant rain. He could see the laughing face of the moon, which had been tickled by the stars; a comet dashing hurriedly through the sky to be there on time for an important date. He was floating in air; no, he was flying free like a bird.

"You haven't drunk your coffee, Sir," came the voice of the waiter, rudely waking him up, and snatching him out of his heavenly dream.

"It has been an hour already. The coffee must be cold now. Do you want me to get you another one?"

"No, thank you," he paid the waiter for the coffee, and walked away leaving the waiter shaking his head, and wide mouthed with astonishment.

When he reached his brother's house, he went straight to the guest room and flung himself, fully clothed, on the bed. He just laughed loudly. He thanked his excellency, the minister, for allowing him to have those nice moments of daydreaming. He was a strong believer in the saying, that there is a silver lining in every dark cloud. A verse in Quran says, "maybe you hate something which is in fact good for you, and you may like something, which is in fact bad for you." Now he felt free, just like when he dreamt, flying through the air like a free bird, with nothing to worry about. At least he didn't need to deal with corrupt people like the minister and other government officials like him.

"Nothing to worry about," he said to himself, looking in the mirror at his unshaven face. He had no job to go to. How was he going to support himself? How was he going to find another job, with this unfavourable security report on his record. He had no house of his own, and his savings were not anything to talk about. He had to find a source of income, and quickly; but had no idea what to do, as he was totally unprepared for this totally unexpected situation. His brother didn't offer any suggestions apart from, "don't worry, something will come up, inshallah."

Dr Omer remembered that just before leaving the Blue Nile province he was asked to head an investigative committee, looking into some provisions disappearing from the stocks. He had already completed the investigation and written the report, which he was supposed to present to the national director of refugees' affairs.

He went over the report and made a few corrections, and headed to the Director's office. The Director welcomed him warmly, and discussed the report in a lot of detail. He thanked Dr Omer for an excellent and comprehensive report.

"By the way, could I arrange for you to have a couple of weeks off from your work, to come and help me deal with the World Health Organization representatives who will be coming in a couple of days' time. Would this be alright with you? I know it is short notice, but I really need your help."

"I can start now if you like." Dr Omer then told him what had happened with the Minister of Health and the fact that now he was unemployed.

"Very sorry to hear that, but I must admit, I am also happy that you are immediately available to help. I know this sounds very selfish of me, and please don't take any offence".

"Not at all, I am also happy that I will be having something to do. I will need a car and a furnished accommodation though."

"That can be arranged. When you come after the weekend, everything will be ready and of course, you will be paid handsomely."

"Thank you very much, indeed. See you next week then."

"Yes. Inshallah."

What happened today, convinced Dr Omer, that what the minister did was for the better, and more good news was on the way. On the way home, Dr Omer bought some fruits and chocolates as a kind of celebration, for his new temporary job. He decided not to tell his brother, about what happened today but will keep it a surprise.

"How was your day?" asked his brother, not expecting to hear any good news.

"It was fine, alhamdulillah. I submitted a report of an investigation to the director, and he was very pleased with it. He didn't even know that I am unemployed now."

"Why didn't you tell him, he might help you find a job?" his brother asked impatiently.

"They are all the same. He also must have received a copy of the security report about me." Dr Omer replied hopelessly.

"Something will come up, inshallah." Dr Omer just rolled his eyes.

That evening, and over the weekend, he started reading some reports about refugees in the Blue Nile province in particular, and Sudan in general to refresh his memory and be ready when he meets with the director and his guests. He couldn't imagine himself without a job for any length of time, he would definitely go crazy. There would be no purpose in life, nothing to look forward to. There would only be an endless vacuum and emptiness. That is why he accepted this temporary job, just to fill the vacuum, while looking for something more substantial. His thoughts went to those who were made redundant by this regime, just because they didn't belong to the Muslim Brothers' organization. These unfortunate people had no prospect of finding a job, because of the security report hanging around their necks. They were not even allowed to leave the country and seek employment abroad; that was grossly unfair. Most of these people were able, civil servants, whose absence would damage the civil service, and negatively affect its performance, to the detriment of the smooth running of government. But according to the doctrine of the Muslim Brothers, affiliation, and allegiance are more important than knowledge, and performance. This made Dr Omer angry, confused, and perplexed. How could anyone put his personal gains above those of his country? Would he be able to work with these people, and not criticise their ways, and get into trouble? Now he was not sure, if he could work in Sudan in any capacity, as long as these people were in power. But he didn't want to work abroad, as Sudan needed him and he had a lot to offer, to improve life of his fellow Sudanese. He found himself between a rock and a hard place; two choices, each one worse than the other. He needed to think, and think hard of a way out of this conundrum. His options were limited at the moment, but he mustn't despair or lose sight of hope.

Dr Omer had a nice cup of morning coffee with the director in his vast office, and wondered if this coffee was also sent to the director from Sri Lanka.

"The driver will take you, in your car, to your residence," said the director gleefully. "Please take a couple of days to relax and get used to the place and I will see you here on Wednesday."

"Thank you very much. That was really quick." The director must have needed him badly, to get all these done in such a short time. He must be one of those people, who had been appointed, just because they belonged to the Muslim Brothers' group, but they were not up to the task, Dr Omer thought to himself, "I will be doing all the work, and he will take the credit."

The car stopped in front of a nice multi-storey building, in one of the posh neighbourhoods in the city.

"This is Dr Omer who will be staying in flat 402," the driver addressed the immaculately dressed security guard.

"Welcome, Dr Omer. These are the keys to your flat, and this is the electronic card to access the building and the car park. Your parking place, which is in basement one, will carry the same number as your flat. In the flat, you will find a booklet of rules and regulations and safety instructions. Please read that carefully, as it is very important. I wish you a very happy stay. Oh, my name is Ali, and I am always here to help."

Dr Omer thanked the security guard, and then drove his car to basement one. He noticed that all the parked cars were of the expensive type and very clean.

402, was a two-bedroom flat. On the coffee table, in the big reception room, there were flowers, artistically arranged in a glass vase, with a welcome card nestled there. The kitchen had all the necessary appliances. The fridge was teeming with fruits, vegetables, milk, juice, and even butter, and cheese. Cupboards are heaving with all that was needed to cook a delicious meal. Both bedrooms were en suite, and with fitted wardrobes. There were stacks of towels in the bathroom, and the instruction booklet mentioned a washing service, which Dr Omer assumed was free. House-keeping service was included, not to mention the central air conditioning.

This was a first-class accommodation, Dr Omer would never have dreamt of. He wondered what sort of luxury, people in higher places were immersed in. It must be something unimaginable.

"What sort of people lives here?" he asked the security guard, on his way out of the building.

"We are not allowed to say who is living in the building. Sorry."

"That is fine; just wanted to know my neighbours."

Dr Omer noticed that the security around the building was very tight, and concluded that some dignitaries lived there, or may be foreigners of some description. Anyway, he decided to mind his own business and keep a low profile.

He drove his car to his brother's house, and went straight to the guest room to soak in all that had happened to him today. Now he had a first-class accommodation, a car, and a job, albeit temporary. Few days ago, he had nothing. The last few days had been a roller coaster ride, as far as he was concerned.

"Whose car was that?" exclaimed his brother, when he saw nobody else in the room,

"It is my car," answered Dr Omer, still reading the newspaper.

"How come?"

His brother listened to the story with a mixture of disbelief and relief.

"I told you something will come up," he said with a grin of confidence, as if he could see into the future and then added, "So, what after this temporary job ends?"

"I am sure something will come up." They both laughed.

"*I will be moving to this place tomorrow morning, and will start the job the day after.*"

"*Can I go with you later to see the place?*" *Listening to your description, I cannot wait till the weekend.*"

"*Yes, we can. I also want to do a little bit of shopping, and I am sure you can help me with that, you being the local boy.*"

It was a lovely Wednesday morning, when Dr Omer was driving to his first working day as the director's advisor. It was sunny as usual, and at this time of the morning, the sun gives you warmth without making you hot and sweaty. Flowers in the balconies were blooming with appreciation, and the birds were singing their melodies with thanks and delight. People seemed to be happy, and in a good mood. Even the stray dogs looked friendly, and sedate. It seemed everyone was happy for Dr Omer. He felt important, and rich in this expensive car, and he decided to enjoy it as long as it lasted.

Dr Omer liked the job for more reasons than one. It allowed him to rub shoulders with important people from the WHO, and UN, and other international organizations, which might open doors for him in the job market. The director was totally dependent on him, when it came to dealing with these international teams. He had the knowledge, and all the information they needed at his fingertips, and they were very impressed by that. He was being paid handsomely, and living a luxurious life.

"*I don't know what I would have done without you. You have been a great help to me, during the last two months or so.*"

"*Thank you, for giving me the chance to help. I find the job very interesting and enjoyable.*"

"*As you might have noticed, the number of teams visiting us is almost coming to a trickle, and I expect that there will be no more teams by the end of this month.*"

Dr Omer kept quiet, but knew what the director was trying to say.

"*So, by the end of this month, your job contract will sadly terminate, but I will be more than happy to help you find a suitable post.*"

"Thank you very much, for the offer. I will let you know if I need help."

"You are welcome, anytime."

Till the end of the month, there was hardly any work; only one team came, and the director dealt with them himself, as it involved management issues and had nothing to do with the nitty gritty of refugees' health. Still, Dr Omer went to the office every morning, had coffee, read the newspapers, chatted with others about nothing in particular, and then went home at the end of the day.

Coming out of the lift, Dr Omer met an old friend, and invited him to his flat.

"Just imagine meeting you here suddenly after all this time."

"I know. It is a crazy world. What are you doing here anyway," asked his friend.

"It is a long story, but basically, for the last three months I have been working as an advisor to the Director, and my job will finish at the end of this month, then I will be available for offers."

"Would you be interested in a job in Saudi Ministry of Health, in the public health sector?"

"To be honest, I will consider anything at the moment. I was not looking for a job here. Tell me more about this job."

"Someone told me about it yesterday, and they are looking for a suitable candidate. I can ring them later, and arrange a meeting with them, so you can hear the details from the horse's mouth."

"Yes. That is a good idea. My diary is empty. Which flat do you stay in?"

"In flat 308. I will go and phone them now, and will pass by you in the evening, and tell you all about it."

Dr Omer tried to eat something he had cooked the night before, but he just couldn't. He had put too much salt. In the end, he had to settle for a tuna, and cucumber sandwich, which he enjoyed for its simplicity.

He kind of liked the idea of going to Saudi Arabia. Loads of money, he would imagine. He had no idea, what life in Saudi was like. He had never thought of working anywhere outside Sudan. His people should be the ones to benefit from his expertise, and knowledge, after all they were the ones who had paid for his education, and training. Now things were different with these Muslim Brothers in power, life could be hell, if you were not one of them, as he had found out in the last few weeks. Corruption was rife, incompetent people were at the helm of governmental departments, and a complete disregard for human rights, was the norm. Dr Omer could not work in such an environment, and the Saudi option seemed to have come at the right time. He would go for it, if it materialised.

"This guy will see you this Thursday morning, at 9 am. Oh, this tea is really nice. Where do you get it from?"

Dr Omer was tempted to say, from Sri Lanka.

"Who is this guy?"

"He is the public health chief in the Ministry of Health, of the Kingdom of Saudi Arabia. He is here to attend a conference, on child health and children's vaccination programme. He is flying back the same evening. You need to prepare your CV, and read about public health problems in southern Saudi Arabia."

"Will he present any paper in this conference?"

"Yes. He will actually present two. I have a copy of both of them."

"I will go over them, and I am sure the contents will come handy when I meet with him."

"He will be impressed, when you tell him the things he wants to hear, but this apart, I think you are the right man for the job, and they will be very fortunate to have you."

"Thank you very much. I will go with you to your flat to take the copies, if that is ok with you. I need to read these papers in detail."

One of the papers was about the prevalence of childhood diseases in southern provinces of Saudi Arabia, and the other one was about the effect of childhood vaccination programme, on the incidence of childhood diseases. They were both well-written papers, and gave a good insight about the situation of childhood diseases in Saudi Arabia. For Dr Omer, doing epidemiological studies, and planning, and executing a vaccination programme was second nature. He had done this successfully in Darfur, and the Blue Nile provinces with excellent results. He felt very confident about this job, and considered it his.

The guy was a middle-aged gentleman, of average build, donned in a snow-white kandura, with a head gear to match; a Rolex watch on his left wrist, and a massive gold ring to go with it. Dr Omer wondered, if he would ever be that filthy rich, and afford such luxury. The answer came swiftly from within him, in the form of a shake of the head.

"Welcome Dr Omer. Please have a seat." This was said with an air of formality.

"Thank you very much." Dr Omer sank into a low, but comfortable armchair wondering how he was going to get out of it later.

After some pleasantries, Dr Omer handed him his CV, and gave him a brief preview of his qualifications and experience.

"Do you have any questions," the guy asked after thirty minutes of interviewing.

"No. Not at the moment."

"Well, I am very impressed. I am offering you this job, and a formal contract will be sent to you. When would you be able to start if everything else is equal?"

Dr Omer just realized, that this was the first time he had faced a one-man panel interview. Was he going to work under a dictator? The thought instilled some discomfort in him, making him shift in his chair. Such an important decision was taken by one person! Surely other stakeholders would have liked to get involved.

"Thank you very much for the offer. Will wait to see the details of the contract, and will be able to start in six weeks, if everything else is equal" He had no idea what this "if everything else is equal" meant.

Dr Omer met the director in his office on the last day of his temporary employment, and went over a few things with him. When he surrendered the car key, the director told him he could keep the car, and the flat for another week, but bear the fuel bill. Dr Omer thanked him, and left with the promise that he would get in touch, if he needed anything.

Chapter 16

WORKING ABROAD

*T*he contract stipulated that Dr Omer would be responsible for setting up, and executing children's vaccination programmes, for the whole of Saudi Arabia with special emphasis on Polio. He would be based in Riyadh. It was an open-ended employment, and the money was good too. He sent back the signed contract, and started the preparations to move to Saudi Arabia.

In September 1989, Dr Omer arrived in Riyadh with his wife, and three kids. Riyadh is a big city, although from the air it appears like a small carbuncle on the face of the vast desert; With wide streets, big American cars with big engines, and cheap petrol. You won't see a woman behind the wheel, they are simply not allowed to drive. One can see men of different nationalities. Women are rarely seen on the streets, but always in a black Abaya, and with the face completely hidden behind a thin black veil, through which you can still make out some beautiful eyes, if you are given a chance to stare long enough. But now things have changed. It is not obligatory for women to cover up, and not only that, but the famous singer Jennifer Lopez also sang on stage in Jeddah wearing an outfit, which left nothing to the imagination, making the audience go crazy in the process, with young men throwing their head gear high in the air, as an expression of their love for her body, or might be for her art, which they might have heard for the first time.

There is a glut of mosques, with the shops closing, and the streets emptying at prayer times. Everyone has to go, and say their prayer either in the mosque or at home. Non-compliance earns you a stern rebuke, painful lashes by special police, or even arrest. Now, these special police have been disbanded, and it is commonplace to find people loitering in the streets, and the shops wide open at prayer times. *The call for prayer comes at the same time from all the mosques through loudspeakers pitched at the top of the minarets, and seems to cancel all other noises and sounds. The day is usually planned around prayer times, like I will see you after Asr prayer.*

The sun never breaks its promise of making an appearance every morning, from the eastern side of the city. It is hot to the point of being uncomfortable. Airconditioning is a must during most of the year. It can also be cold in the short winter. Dry cold which you can feel in your bones. Rainy season usually lasts for only a couple of weeks.

Dr Omer started the job he knew well and loved very much. He assembled and trained the teams, laid out the policies and protocols, summoned the logistical support, made a timetable for every step, and made sure that the budget was adequate, and the funds were readily available, and the staff paid well.

The vaccination program then started in earnest. Dr Omer kept all the staff happy, and content by providing good working conditions, empowering the team leaders, continuous training, insisting on regular field reports, and feedback, and accurate stats.

In less than three years, the Kingdom of Saudi Arabia was declared Polio free by the World Health Organization (WHO). It also acknowledged that the incidence of childhood diseases like measles, whooping cough, mumps, diphtheria, and others had decreased significantly. That was amazing. Everybody was talking about it, and it was all over the news. It is a privilege that a country becomes Polio free, as it is a good indicator, that the country is doing fine as far as health management is concerned. That is why Saudi Arabia publicised this widely, both nationally and internationally. World Health Organization (WHO) recognised this as an achievement of epic proportions, specially that it had been done in such a short span of time, and in such a vast country. Dr Omer was the one who presided over this achievement, and was so proud of himself. It would definitely look very impressive on his CV, and would come handy for promotions, or getting another job.

Dr Omer stayed in Saudi Arabia till 1999, when he received a phone call from the WHO representative.

"Hello Dr Omer. I am the WHO representative in Iraq. I got your number from our office in Riyadh."

"Hello. What can I do for you?"

"You see, we need someone to come to Iraq for a month or so, to deal with the recent Polio outbreak there. You have been highly recommended by our regional office, who have been following the excellent work you have been doing in Saudi Arabia, in the field of vaccination and Polio control." There was a long period of silence, as Dr Omer was not expecting something like this.

"Is it safe in Iraq?" He asked impulsively.

"As you know, there are troubles here and there, but usually the WHO staff is well protected, and I am sure with time, things will become better."

"For how long have you been in Iraq?"

"Five years."

"With your family?"

"I thought, I am the one who is supposed to ask the questions," said the guy, laughingly, "My wife and two kids, aged 7 and 4 years, are all very happy, and enjoying life in Iraq."

"I am sure you know all about "oil for food programme" which was imposed on Iraq after the war," he added.

"Yes, I do."

"That, in a way, affects our operations, as the budget comes from there."

Dr Omer felt, as if he had already got the job, if this guy was discussing such issues with him.

'And what has this to do with me now?" He meant this as a leading question.

"It has everything to do with you, Dr Omer. We have already decided, you are the man for the job pending your approval."

"Well, I need to think it over. I need to have a word with my wife and family."

"Please take all the time in the world, but we do need you as soon as possible. What is your gut feeling about it?"

"Favourable."

"These are my contact details; please let me know as soon as you have decided. Also, if you have any questions, please do ask. I will send you the contract, and I hope you will be a part of our team soon."

"OK, that is fine. Thank you."

From his own investigation, Dr Omer knew that this job would most probably be a long term, or even a permanent one with the WHO. The contract was good, and the salary was much more than what he would hope for, and it was going to be paid in US dollars. He was just a bit worried about the emphasis on security throughout the contract, a feeling shared by his wife. This uneasy feeling was compounded by the inflammatory rhetoric coming out of Washington, and Baghdad. He and his wife toiled over the decision, but in the end decided to accept the offer. They were encouraged and reassured by some of their friends, who had lived and worked in Iraq for a few years. It would be a totally new experience for them in the circumstances. Iraq was in turmoil and the future was uncertain. Children's education prospects were good though. Provisions were made for children of those working for international organizations, and there were so many of them in Iraq.

Who would have thought Dr Omer will one day work in countries other than Sudan? It dawned on him that he might be going from one country to another, for the rest of his life. The thought made him sad and angry. What about his children? Will they be able to cope? And will their future be affected in a negative way? Every time they move to another country they will miss their friends, interrupt their routine, and the whole thing would be very unsettling for them. He tried to convince himself, that there is a silver lining to this dark cloud of gloom. He was going to have a good and well-paid job; his children might benefit from exposure to different cultures, which will enrich their lives. He himself will gain a lot of experience, and knowledge, which he will, hopefully, one day apply in Sudan. Of course, this will be dependent on the Muslim Brothers relinquishing power. Like Dr

Omer, many Sudanese professionals had chosen to stay and work abroad rather than work in Sudan with these people in charge.

To go to Iraq, Dr Omer flew to Alexandria, and then to Amman in Jordan. There were no direct flights to Baghdad, as Iraq was declared as a no-fly zone by the Americans, after the war of 1990. From Amman, he took a taxi to Baghdad, an arduous and tiring journey.

Before the 1990 war on Iraq, which was led mainly by the US, and Britain, and other western nations (falsely called international coalition), Iraq was a rich country, exporting millions of barrels of oil a day, its citizens lived a decent life; there was excellent infra-structure, free education and healthcare for all, and well-run governmental departments. It was ruled by a dictator, Sadam Hussain, but this was a matter for the Iraqis to deal with, and was not anybody else's business.

Almutanabi street in Baghdad is famous for its many bookshops, libraries, book stalls, cafes, where poets and writers, meet and chat. Here you can find any book you fancy; you can even find original copies of famous books and volumes. People reckon, that if you put these libraries, and bookshops, and stalls together, they might be containing more books than the library of the congress.

Almutanabi was a famous and well-known poet, born in Iraq in 915, and died in 965. He lived in Iraq, Syria, and Egypt, praising rulers of these countries, for money and privilege. He is considered by many, as the greatest Arab poet who ever lived. I myself think the same, and I enjoy his poetry very much, and for some time now, I read some verses from his book every night before I go to bed.

After the 1990 war, US and Britain imposed stiff sanctions on Iraq, and introduced "oil for food program," through which Iraqi oil will be sold, and the money thus generated will be put in a special account in the United Nations, which will be responsible for buying food for the Iraqis. Just imagine, your own money controlled by somebody else, who will decide what to buy and not buy for you. This special United Nations account is allowed to buy food only, and nothing else. No cars, no motorbikes, or bicycles, no aeroplanes, no spare parts of any kind, no hospital equipment, no agricultural machinery, no fertilizers, nothing, only food. In 1999, the newest car in Iraq was at least ten years old. They were not even allowed to buy certain medications, like Glycerine Trinitrate (GTN), which is an important medicine for those patients, who suffer from ischaemic heart disease. The reason for this being, that it might be used to make explosives; but, of course, it was of no consequence for the Americans and the British, if Iraqi patients suffered pain or died. Another imposed sanction was, against importing BCG vaccine. This vaccine is used mainly in children against tuberculosis. The reason for the sanction, according to the Americans and the British, was that BCG might be used by the Iraqis as a biological weapon. This had led to the resurgence of the deadly disease of tuberculosis, among the Iraqis with devastating consequences. Iraqi children dying from the disease as a result, did not concern the Americans and the British and might have been considered as a price worth paying. It is worth mentioning, that tuberculosis in children was unknown in Iraq before the 1990 war.

After the 1990 war, power outages were a common occurrence due to lack of spare parts for the power plants and power stations. Also, stand-by electricity generators stopped working for the same reason. Sanitation system broke down, resulting in sewage contaminating drinking water and food; refuse collection cars slowly went out of action, leading to accumulation of garbage in the streets. These combined, resulted in a sharp increase in the incidence of communicable diseases like hepatitis, typhoid, diarrhoea, and others. The Americans and the British said, "This has nothing to do with us, it is Saddam Hussain's fault!" And what do you expect; they are the champions of human rights around the world. Big joke!

Now, the outbreak of Polio, a good barometer for the deterioration of healthcare standards, was the last straw. Things had reached a new low.

When Dr Omer arrived in Baghdad and started working, he was shocked by the state of affairs there. Due to repeated electricity outages, and out of order stand-by generators, most of the Polio vaccines were rendered ineffective. When he was out doing field work and meeting with families, he discovered that records had been falsified. Children who didn't receive any vaccine, were recorded as vaccinated. Some children were not even registered.

Dr Omer decided to start from scratch. His experience came handy in these situations. He assembled teams, to assess the situation by doing more field work. He made arrangements, to make sure that the vaccine was kept refrigerated all the time, and that all the logistical support was available and ready. The vaccination programme then started in earnest. As his mission was for a couple of months only, he wanted to lay down a strong base, and clear protocols, so that this work would be completed successfully.

Towards the end of the first month in Iraq, he was told that his job with the WHO will be a permanent post, and that he will continue to work in Iraq, but might be sent to other countries, if the need arises. He was assured, though, that he will be staying here for at least five years, as there was still a lot to be done, considering the deteriorating situation of the healthcare sector.

Dr Omer started planning, to bring his wife and kids to Iraq. They flew to Egypt, and from there to Amman in Jordan, where Dr Omer met them. They had to travel by road to Baghdad, as Iraq was declared as a no-fly zone by the Americans and the British. People suffered hardships, but so what!

Before the 1990 war, the Iraqi Dinar could buy more than three US dollars. Now in 1999, one US dollar could buy 2000 Iraqi dinars. Wow! This shows the scale of deterioration, which was caused by the war, and sanctions, and the many resolutions put in place by the Americans and the British, through the United Nations and the Security Council, to destroy this great nation.

In a little over two years, Iraq was again declared a Polio free country by the World Health Organization (WHO). This was recognised as a significant achievement in such a record time, and in such circumstances. Dr Omer acquired a reputation as the Polio basher. This is what those in the public health sector called him.

The war against Polio was not over. Continuous surveillance, and public awareness were important. Reporting of any remotely suspected cases was mandatory, as was the vaccination of newly born babies. *No birth certificate was issued, unless the baby already had the vaccination. The monthly food rations were not approved, unless the birth certificate was presented. This policy had increased the compliance with the Polio and other childhood vaccinations.*

The family were enjoying the life in Baghdad. The schools were good and of high standards, and the children made friends from different nationalities, and it was usual for them to come up with words, and sentences, from different languages like French, Spanish, Urdu, and others. Mixing and interacting with other cultures, would benefit them in their adult life, and enrich their souls and improve their understanding of humanity. This same benefit would rub onto Dr Omer and his wife.

The cost of living was very low, and things were very cheap. A whole week's grocery shopping would cost around ten dollars only. You could rent a four-bedroom villa for a mere 300 US dollars, per calendar month. Petrol was cheap, and mostly provided by the WHO for its employees. The salary of the WHO employees was paid in US dollars, a fact, which made it possible for them to live a somewhat luxurious life, if we consider the ridiculously high exchange rate between the dollar and the Iraqi dinar.

Life went on without any significant problems to the point of becoming monotonous. Then BANG! September Eleven attack in 2001. This was planned by the Al Qaeda group, led by Osama bin Laden, in Afghanistan. On that day four aeroplanes flying over eastern United States were hijacked. They were then used as giant, guided missiles to crash into landmark buildings in New York and Washington. Two planes crashed into the twin towers of the World Trade Centre in New York. The first hit the North Tower at 12:46 GMT, and the second smashed into the South Tower at 13:03 GMT. This was broadcasted live on TV around the world and watched by millions. In less than two hours 110-storey towers collapsed in massive clouds of dust.

At 13:37 GMT, the third plane destroyed the western face of the Pentagon, the giant headquarters of the US military just outside the nation's capital, Washington DC.

The fourth plane crashed in a field in Pennsylvania at 14:03 GMT, after passengers fought back. This plane was thought to be intended for the Capitol Building in Washington DC.

Almost 3000 people died in these attacks. The attack remains one of the most traumatic events for the American people. It was a catastrophe, and a tragedy in an ever increasingly turbulent, and violent, and an unjust world.

Shortly after the September eleven attack, the United States declared a War on Terror, and subsequently led, with Britain, a multinational military force and invaded Afghanistan on the 7th of October 2001. It was a multinational force just in name, for the United States and Britain to legitimize the unlawful invasion of a sovereign country.

⸻◈⸻

Chapter 17

THE INVASION OF IRAQ

While The War on Terror was going on in Afghanistan, America and Britain started to talk about Iraq's possession of Weapons of Mass Destruction (WMD). The British Prime Minister, Tony Blair, stood in the House of Commons, and lied through his teeth to his MPs, to the British people, and to the whole world and said, "Our intelligence services have confirmed beyond any doubt, that Saddam Hussain has chemical and biological weapons, and in 48 hours, he is going to possess nuclear weapons. We have to stop him, and liberate the people of Iraq. This is part and parcel of the War against Terror. We have to act quickly, and decisively to protect our national security, and to prevent future catastrophes."

The American Secretary of State, General Colin Powell, stood at the podium in the United Nations Assembly, and lied through his teeth, to the whole world saying, that their intelligence services confirmed beyond any doubt, that Iraq had Weapons of Mass Destruction (WMD). He projected some fuzzy photos of trucks, and buildings, as proof, even though the United Nations inspection team, led by Hans Blix, had declared, that they found no evidence of Weapons of Mass Destruction in Iraq.

In spite of the report by the United Nations inspection team, and in spite of the wide opposition to the idea of the invasion around the world, the United States and Britain invaded Iraq on the 20th of March 2003. Up to 45000 Iraqi troops were killed in combat, and hundreds of thousands of Iraqi civilians were killed during the invasion, and later during the occupation.

Soon after the invasion, the Coalition Provisional Authority (CPA) was established, as the first in successive authorities to govern occupied Iraq.

The Iraqi army, the police force, security services, were all disbanded, without any alternative put in place. Senior civil servants disappeared, as they all belonged to the Arab Socialist Ba'ath party, also known simply as Ba'ath party. The country descended into chaos. The palaces, the museums, the banks, governmental buildings, businesses, and various other institutions were looted. Thousands of rare historical artefacts were stolen, and taken outside the country. What a great shame!

Dr Omer was evacuated to Amman in Jordan, a day before the invasion, while his family was evacuated in November 2002. They were sad, they had to move again, and disrupt their lives. Most of their friends had been evacuated too. No body knew how long this situation was going to last, or what the next move was. But they knew one thing; the Americans and the British were wrong to invade a sovereign country. They also knew that Iraq will never be the same again.

The first stage of the war, formally ended on 1st of May 2003, when President George Bush declared the "end of major combat operations." WHO personnel in Amman started exploring the possibility of going back to Iraq, and resume its mission there. Staff security was a major issue. They started talking to the Coalition Provisional Authority (CPA), about the logistics of doing so. The CPA was a new authority, and people doubted if the health of Iraqis was a priority for it.

It was agreed, that WHO could resume its operations in Iraq towards the end of May. Many Iraqis had crossed into Jordan, before the invasion. Dr Omer was able to recruit some of these Iraqis, and some who had already worked with him.

After the invasion, things were different. A lot of roads were unpassable, and most of the bridges were damaged, or completely destroyed. Energy supplies were wanting. The movement of people was restricted, with multiple check points along the way. Security was non-existent, random shootings, and arrests were commonplace. Sectarian violence erupted, and neighbours turned against each other. "Oil for food" programme was cancelled, and now the CPA was in full control. The Americans and the British were effectively running the country now. It was said, that the oil revenue was used to pay for the salaries of their soldiers, and the inflated pay packet of the CPA employees, and other expenses incurred; Iraq got the leftovers.

Healthcare infrastructure was in ruins, some health centres, and hospitals were destroyed or looted. Most of the healthcare staff, except a few, had left, either of their own volition, or forcibly removed, because they were members of the Ba'ath party, or because of security concern, or just disappeared, or were killed in the midst of the chaos.

With the "Oil for Food programme," now cancelled, the WHO had to negotiate with the Coalition Provisional Authority (CPA), whose priorities were different from those of the United Nations. They also had to deal with the 606 Committee, made up of members from the invading countries, which decided what medicine, or medical equipment was allowed to be imported into the country. This made life much more difficult.

Despite all the difficulties and challenges, the WHO managed to get the health services to meet the basic needs of the population, at least in Baghdad. Field work, and vaccination programme limped on. All the ingredients were there for Polio, and other childhood diseases to make a comeback, but Dr Omer and team were determined to close all the doors and avenues. It wasn't as easy as before the invasion. In fact, it was a lot more difficult. There were problems, like less staff who were also not as experienced, frequent absenteeism due to lack of security, and frequent enforcement of curfews.

Life went on, but with a new reality, and completely different way of life. Roads were dirty with dried human blood, and unpassable in the best of times. This was compounded by many checkpoints, and frequent curfews. Thousands of pink-faced, trigger-happy soldiers, in their full military fatigues roamed the streets, speaking a strange language, and arresting people at will.

Non-stop sound of gunfire was commonplace to the point, that people got used to it. They commented on it, only if it ever got quieter. Deafening explosions were a daily occurrence, and could be heard across the city. There was always smoke, billowing from somewhere, and hanging over Baghdad. The sun, sometimes, found it difficult to get through. You could feel sadness, and resentment everywhere.

You could smell the injustice and horror. Death was in the air, and everybody was breathing it. Killing on sectarian lines was rife. If you were a Sunni, passing through a Shia roadblock, then you were singled out, and killed, and vice versa. Iraqi resistance groups were killing American soldiers left, right, and centre. Soldiers of the invading countries were considered as legitimate targets, as they had no business being there in the first place. Call it resistance to occupation, self-defence, or whatever you want to call it.

Prisons were full to the brim. The majority of the inmates didn't know why they were there, and what they had done to get arrested, and when, if ever, they were going to be released, and set free. Bored soldiers, doubling as prison guards, used to torture the inmates, as a pastime activity to kill boredom, and in the process, some prisoners would be killed. This was entered in the records as natural death. A healthy, young man, dying a natural death in prison, was normal at that time, under that administration.

The value of the Iraqi Dinar was now so low, that it was not worth the paper it was printed on. If you found an Iraqi Dinar on the floor, it was a waste of time, bending down to pick it up. Salaries were not paid on time, and most families struggled to make ends meet. Children went hungry, and signs of malnutrition started to be noticeable in both children, and adults.

Water borne diseases, affecting mostly children, were commonplace. This is because, most of the water sanitation plants and sewage systems were deliberately destroyed by the invading powers led by the Americans and the British. You didn't have to be a military expert to see, that destroying the water sanitation plants, and sewage systems had no strategic, military significance, and was done as a part of destroying the infrastructure of the country, and punishing the Iraqi people for being unfriendly. Mortality, and morbidity from these diseases were high, especially because the healthcare systems were also severely compromised by the invasion, and the sanctions.

Life was not enjoyable in Baghdad anymore. No safety, no enjoyment. A bomb could explode near you anytime, a stray bullet could hit you while you were standing at your window, a trigger-happy, frightened soldier might shoot you while you were reaching into your pockets for your car keys, considering you a threat. He followed the policy of, "shoot first and then ask questions." Saying the wrong thing at the wrong time might be fatal. You could not trust anyone. Your movements were curtailed. You stayed inside the house, most of the time behind locked doors with no entertainment. Weather was boiling hot, and power outages were frequent, and continued for a long time. Piped water was cloudy in colour and untreated. You needed to boil it, to avoid developing diarrhoea and other water borne diseases.

Despite the stressful life, and difficult conditions, United Nations, and WHO teams carried on working, and risking their lives for the sake of humanity. They continued to make progress in improving the dire situation. Of course, the majority of Iraqis welcomed the United Nations' teams, as they could see the good job they were doing for them. Unfortunately, other Iraqis considered these organizations, as a part of the invading forces, and had to be treated as such. This put the employees of these organizations, at a greater danger.

⇠⋙❖⋘⇢

Chapter 18

THE EXPLOSION

A wreath laid at the annihilated Canal Hotel with a banner saying "Iraqi people refused the criminal and terrorist attack on the UN building in Baghdad."

This photo is courtesy of Mr Walid Salih, formerly finance and admin officer WHO office, Baghdad

A Close up showing the level of devastation caused by the explosion. 23people died, more than a 100 injured.

This photo is courtesy of Mr Walid Salih, formerly finance and admin officer WHO office, Baghdad

*T*uesday, the 19ᵗʰ of August 2003, seemed like a normal day in Baghdad. The sun rose from the east, as it does every morning, and quickly proceeded westwards, to position itself right overhead in Baghdad. The temperature gauge read 50 degrees Celsius in the shade. Overheated cars stopped by the side of the road, with their bonnets lifted up like sunbathing crocks. The few people, who were roaming the streets, were dashing around with their clothes soaked in sweat. Stray dogs were lying down in front of shops, with their tongues hanging out, waiting for the air conditioners to start working again.*

Traffic lights were not working, and this was causing chaos and traffic jams. The traffic light's metal was twisted by the extreme heat, and the tarmac was melting. The stench from overflowing sewage was unbearable, but after a while you got used to it. This is the process of adaptation. Medics will tell you, it is due to the depletion of the neurotransmitter, which transmits the neural impulse across the synaptic gap, from repeated stimulation. Does this make sense to you? Sorry, that sounded very technical, but whatever it might be, it is a welcome process. This extreme heat, I assume, would have killed some bad bugs; so, it was not all bad news.

On that same Tuesday, the 19ᵗʰ of August 2003, Dr Omer was sitting in his office in the WHO headquarters doing his daily routine work. Deep down he had this unusual feeling, and he felt uncomfortable, but he quickly dismissed that feeling, and carried on with what he was doing.

The phone in his office rang.

"Hello Dr Omer. I am ringing you from the United Nations Headquarters in the Canal Hotel," said the voice.

"Hello there. How can I help?"

"Mr Popal, who is supposed to attend an important meeting today, is, unfortunately, not available and you were nominated to stand in for him. The meeting is about finalizing the UN policy, of how to deal with the new Coalition Provisional Authority (CPA). As you have been involved in the initial discussions, you are our man for this job."

"What time is this meeting?"

"3 p.m. today in Sergio di Mello's office, can you make it?"

"It is a very, short notice, but I suppose I could. In the next couple of hours, I will go over the documents to refresh my memory."

"See you there."

The Canal Hotel was about five kilometres away. It was an L-shaped, three storey building, on the bank of a canal. I don't blame you, if you thought, that this was a romantic location; in fact, this canal was a drainage canal, carrying dirty water, and far removed from romance. The canal provided an ideal place for the breeding of mosquitoes, and emitted the sort of smell, your olfactory receptors wouldn't be happy with. Those living on the banks of the canal, must have suffered sleepless nights from mosquito bites, and recurrent attacks of malaria.

As Dr Omer parked his car at the Canal Hotel, his wife rang him from Riyadh, Saudi Arabia.

"Alsalamualaikum. How are you, all well?"

"Wa Alaikum Alsalam, I am fine, alhamdulillah."

"Are you busy, can I talk?"

"I just arrived at the Canal Hotel, to attend a meeting. Tell me."

"Khartoum University has opened, and Samah has to travel to Khartoum ASAP. Can you change her ticket, Riyadh to Khartoum instead of Riyadh to Amman. Can you do this, before you start the meeting, if possible. These meetings can go on forever, you know."

"I will ring them now and sort this out. Consider it done. Salam to the kids, and the rest of the family. Will ring you after the meeting inshallah."

He went into the hotel, and everything seemed to be normal, nothing out of the ordinary, just more than normal people from the press. He was told, that the meeting was delayed, because Sergio di Mello was in an open-ended news conference. No body knew when it was going to end, and no alternative time for the meeting had been decided. Sergio di Mello was the representative of the Secretary General of the United Nations, and was the most senior. He was there to see for himself, things on the ground, and report back to the Secretary General.

Dr Omer decided to go back to his office, as it was unlikely that the meeting would be held today. He exited the hotel, and walked across the car park, towards his car.

"Hi, Dr Omer," a UNICEF representative greeted him.

"Hi, man. What brought you here?"

"I came to attend this meeting, regarding the policy towards the CPA."

"The meeting has been delayed, and no one knows, when it is going to be convened, that is why I am going back to my office."

"No. The meeting hasn't been cancelled, only the venue was changed. It will start in ten minutes."

"Are you sure?"

"Hundred percent."

Both walked back into the hotel. They sat in a small room, directly below Sergio di Mello's office, on the ground floor. There were four or five people already there, sipping coffee. Dr Omer asked for black tea. The office boy obliged, and he was kind enough to bring some biscuits along. Dr Omer loved biscuits and always quoted the ad, "tea is too wet without one."

While waiting for the rest to arrive, everyone in the room was bent on his phone, checking the latest news and messages.

"There was an explosion in the Green Zone early this morning," one said suddenly.

"Oh, my God! If they can penetrate the Green Zone, then nobody is safe including us here."

"Funny to say, that I always thought, the security around this hotel is not tight enough."

"Don't worry. I don't think the Iraqis will harm people, who are here to help them."

Now everybody was here. The office boy brought coffee, for the last attendee, and before he left the office, BAM, a deafening explosion ripped through the room. But the deafening noise could not be heard, by those at the epicentre of the explosion. The last thing Dr Omer could remember was the office boy leaving the room, and the lady sitting opposite raising the index finger of her right hand, as if about to say something, then everything plunged into darkness. I wonder what she was going to say. That might never be known.

The scene at the hotel was that of complete and utter carnage. That part of the hotel was almost completely obliterated. People were running in all directions like headless chicken. Others were shouting, some were walking, wounded, crying in pain and despair. Rubble, broken glass, blood and body parts, and American soldiers were everywhere. Thick smoke, fear, and the smell of death dominated the scene. Some were sitting with their heads in their hands, in total shock.

The military was trying to make sense of the situation, and reach a stage of organized chaos. They established a cordon around the scene, and searched the location to make sure there were no other incendiary devices.

Medics, also from the military, were trying to establish a system of field triage, to deal with the victims in the midst of all the chaos.

Dr David Nabarro Director of Emergency Action in Crisis, who was in Iraq to establish the emergency system plan, to deal with the consequences of the American/British invasion, was present at the scene and taking active part in field triaging. He himself suffered only minor cuts and bruises.

"Leave this one, I don't think we can do anything for him," said one of the medics pointing to a man, whose intestines were hanging out, and both his legs were missing.

"We need to evacuate this patient urgently," another medic shouted, while applying a torniquet and bandages to the leg of a patient, who also has a head injury.

"Could we please arrange to evacuate this patient now?" shouted Dr Nabarro authoritatively, pointing in the direction of three victims, lying side by side.

"Which one are you talking about?" asked one of the transfer crew.

"That one who lost his face. He only has head and facial injuries, but his airway is in danger of being compromised if we don't act fast.

He is breathing at the moment, but he is unconscious and might need securing of his airway as a matter of urgency."

Medics leant down beside that faceless victim, inserted some tubes, and needles, and took him away to a waiting helicopter, which then rumbled away.

It was later established, that a truck packed with explosives was driven through the gates of the hotel and detonated. It was a huge explosion, heard across Baghdad. Twenty-three people died at the scene, including Mr Sergio di Mello, and scores were injured, most of them seriously. Structural damage was massive.

ISIS claimed responsibility, and their main target was Sergio di Mello, as he was instrumental in the conclusion of East Timur case, which they didn't approve of. They were also targeting the invading forces and the United Nations' organisations and personnel. They wanted to drive all these infidels out of Iraq. They had carried out a lot of suicide bombings, which are very difficult to guard against. Although they are more active in the Northwestern part of Iraq, Baghdad is not immune. They have a lot of followers.

Dr Omer's wife, Thuria, rang him from Saudi Arabia to ask, if he had changed Samah's tickets. There was no answer even on the tenth call. Might be, he is still in the meeting, she thought. She rang his other phone, which he usually kept in the office. Walid, from admin and finance, answered the phone.

"Hello. This is Walid."

"Walid, this is Thuria. Is he, is... is.. he ok," came the trembling voice, through the receiver. Walid didn't know what to say, because he was not really sure what Dr Omer's situation was. There was a long, painful silence.

"Tell me please. Is he dead? He is dead, isn't he? Isn't he?"

"Please calm down, and listen to me. He was in the Canal Hotel, and he was injured in the explosion, but his injuries were not bad, and he is receiving treatment. He will be fine. I will ring you again, soon after I get more information."

"Where is he now? Did you see him?"

"Yes, I saw him. He is in the hospital," this was a blatant lie. He hadn't seen him, and had no idea for sure, where he was.

Dr Omer was in coma, when he was airlifted to a military base hospital in Albalad town in Salaheddin province. There he was immediately taken to the operating theatre, and underwent an emergency craniotomy (opening of his skull), to remove a blood clot around his brain. His condition remained critical. He was admitted to the Intensive Care Unit postoperatively.

Casualties kept pouring into the hospital, with all kinds of injuries. This was a military base hospital, and accepted American personnel only. Dr Omer was accepted as an American, and that is why he was here. The name on his wrist badge said, "John Doe," which in the American culture means an unidentified person. He continued to be in coma, and his condition was not improving, but at least he was stable for the moment.

As the hospital, and specially the Intensive Care Unit became overwhelmed and overstretched, it was decided to transfer Dr Omer, and other patients to a hospital in Kuwait. Early the following morning, he was prepared, and airlifted to Kuwait. Soon after arriving there, his condition deteriorated, and he had to have another craniotomy, to evacuate a further blood clot, which had collected on his brain. His coma was not improving, but he could breathe spontaneously.

Back in Baghdad, Walid and Popal came to know, that Dr Omer was airlifted to Albalad Military base Hospital. They drove there to see him. Walid had to ring Thuria, and update her. The drive was not that bad. The United Nations' car could pass through the roadblocks, without much fuss.

"Hi. Can I help you gentlemen?" asked the receptionist, with a well-rehearsed smile on her heavily powdered face.

"We came to know that a friend of ours was transferred to your hospital, from the explosion of the Canal Hotel, and we are wondering, if we can see him or know about his condition?"

"All the patients from the Canal Hotel explosion have been transferred to Kuwait this morning."

"Do you have more details, like names."

"For this, you have to go to Intensive Care reception. Go down the corridor, and it is the second door on your right."

"Thank you."

At the Intensive Care reception, they were met by a nice, cheerful nurse, who confirmed that all the patients had been transferred to Kuwait.

"Do you remember, if one of them is a tall, black guy with a bushy moustache?"

"Yes, one of them fits the description, and by the way, we found this wallet in what remained of his trousers, after he left for Kuwait. Have a look at it, and see if he is your friend."

"Yes. This is our friend. Can we keep it for him?"

"Yes, you can."

Walid and Popal hurriedly left the hospital, realizing that Dr Omer had been mistakenly considered as an American. Thank God nobody looked into his wallet. Otherwise, he wouldn't have been accepted in this hospital, or even evacuated from the disaster scene. Americans look after their own kind only, even in situations like this.

A United Nations Development Programme (UNDP) representative in Kuwait, was asked to confirm that Dr Omer was actually there. He took with him a Sudanese pilot called Tariq, to help in the translation at roadblocks, mainly manned by Arabic speaking Kuwaitis. At the Military field hospital in Kuwait, they were told that they received only dead bodies, and they had some American personnel, who were being prepared for transfer to Germany today. Tariq went inside, and saw Dr Omer with a group of patients, having the final checkup for transfer. He looked fine, apart from being unconscious, and having bandages over his head, and the right side of his face. He looked as if he was asleep.

"Hi man, I know you are from the United Nations, but these guys, who are all Americans, are being transferred to Germany now. How did you get here anyway?"

"We are looking for a friend of ours, who was injured in the Canal Hotel explosion, and we are wondering if he has been evacuated to your hospital."

"All the patients who were transferred to us, are American personnel. I suppose your guy is not American. So, if you could excuse me, please."

The UN representative, and Tariq didn't say anything about the identity of their friend, they knew, that the Americans didn't know that he was not American. They could see, that he was in good hands, and at least knew where he was going to. The evacuation of American personnel usually takes place, to the field hospital in the large American military Airbase in Ramstein. Ramstein Air Base serves as the headquarters of the United States Air Forces, Air Forces Africa, and NATO Allied Air Command, in Europe. Ramstein hosts the largest American community, outside the United States.

Dr Omer's condition didn't improve, and he needed another craniotomy, and evacuation of further clots. He also developed Pseudomonas septicaemia. This is a serious infection in the blood, needs intensive treatment, especially since the Pseudomonas bacteria is usually resistant to many antibiotics.

On the fifth day after the accident, Dr Omer woke up. He felt exhausted and weak. Through a splitting headache, he could see that he was in a strange place. The presence of many nice, and beautiful girls, confused him. For a moment he thought he was in paradise, but he wasn't sure that he had done enough to qualify for it.

"Excuse me. Where am I?" he said in a hardly audible voice. The words were not very clear, due to the injury on the right side of his face.

"You are in a hospital," answered the smiling angel.

"In a hospital? Why am I in a hospital?"

"It is because of the accident. How are you feeling?"

"I have a very severe headache. Please do something about it."

The heavenly angel gave him an injection in his left upper arm, and after a short while, the pain started subsiding. This allowed him to close his eyes, and go to sleep again. He slept deeply, no heavenly dreams though.

"John Doe woke up, and spoke to me. He sounds reasonable. He had a headache, and I gave him a painkiller injection," the nurse told his physician.

"Really? Is he still awake?" responded the physician, with a mixture of disbelief, surprise and hope.

"No. He went back to sleep."

"Oh. Please let me know, immediately, when he wakes up again, whatever the time is."

Back in Saudi Arabia, Thuraya had confirmation from the WHO staff that Dr Omer was in Germany and his condition was not bad, but not good, either. They asked her to prepare to go to Germany, and they would help her with the process. She had to apply for a visa, book a flight, arrange for the kids to be looked after, and decide on things to take with her. She didn't have the foggiest idea, of how long she was going to be there, or if she was going to see the same Omer she knows or someone different. Worry was wearing her down. She hardly slept, and when she did sleep, nightmares attacked her sanity and spoilt those few moments of sleep. She was trying to put on a brave face in the whole situation, and keep herself together, to be a source of strength for her kids.

"Sir, John Doe woke up again. Would you like to come and see him now?"

"Yes. Please keep his notes ready. Please inform the Psychologist of this development, so they can arrange to review him later."

The physician entered the room, and was surprised to find John Doe propped up in bed looking normal, and fully conscious. He was looking around, and seemed to be interested in what was going on in the room. This was the same patient, who had been in coma, for the last five days, had three craniotomies, and everybody had given up on him, and thought he had a life changing injury. There he was, a normal looking human being.

"Good morning. I am your physician, Sergeant Riley and this is Private Stones, your nurse. How are you feeling?"

"I am fine. The nurse told me, that I have been in an accident."

"Yes. That is true."

"What sort of accident? What exactly happened?"

"Will tell you all the details in good time. Now we need some information about you."

"I am starting to have a severe headache, could you please give me something? I also feel very tired."

The nurse gave him a painkiller injection, and he slowly drifted into sleep.

"Private Stone, could you please arrange for him to have an urgent CT scan of his head, repeat his blood tests, and monitor his vital signs, and Glasgow Coma Scale more closely. We need to make sure that he didn't develop any brain abscess, from his previous septicaemia or another blood clot."

"Yes, Sir."

"Ah, and please let me know the results as soon as they come in."

Sergeant Riley walked out of the room perplexed, and confused. He spoke to his colleagues about John Doe, and asked for their opinion, now that all the investigation results were normal. No one came up with a valid explanation.

"Good afternoon. I am your physician, Sergeant Riley. Do you remember me?"

"Yes. You came round this morning."

"How are you feeling now? Any headaches?"

"I am fine, thank you."

"What is your name?"

"Omer Mekki."

"Where are you from?"

"From Sudan."

"Which state?"

"I am from Sudan."

"I know, but which state?"

"I am from Sudan, which is a country in Africa," John Doe said raising his left eyebrow, and angry that this sergeant, with this air of importance around him didn't know what is Sudan and where it is.

"So, you are not American?"

"No. I have never been one."

"What do you do for a living?"

"I work for the WHO."

"Do you remember where you were, last?"

"I was in Iraq, but have no idea, how I ended up here, and what happened to me. Can someone please tell me? By the way, what day is it, or shall I say what month is it?" John Doe responded with a half-smile, that is, only the left side of his face was smiling. The right side of his face had a white bandage saying, "out of order."

"I don't want to overwhelm you, with a lot of details just now; but basically, you were working in Baghdad, when you were involved in an explosion, and were brought here. You have been in coma for the last six days."

Dr Omer's head dropped, and he was silent for a good while. His thoughts went to his family. Did they know, what happened to him, and his whereabouts? He started to feel dizzy, and felt that the headache was coming back, and his stomach churned.

"Wow! I feel like going to sleep, and a bit of a nagging headache."

"Ok. Will leave you to it. Do you think you need a painkiller?"

"I will try to do without it. I don't want to get used to these poisons, but will let you know if the headache becomes unmanageable."

"Will try and come to see you later."

The sergeant exited the room, and went straight to his office, mumbling to himself. He looked at what he jotted down from the interview with John Doe, and shook his head in disbelief. How could this happen, he said to himself.

He picked up the receiver and dialled a number, straightening his back.

"*Good afternoon, Sir. I hope I am not disturbing you,*" *he paused for a little while, and then continued.*

"*Sir, we have a patient in room 5 in the Intensive Care Unit, who has been here for the last five days. He has been in a coma all this time, and woke up yesterday, late afternoon. He was transferred here from Iraq via our military hospital in Kuwait, as an unidentified, American personnel. When I interviewed him today, I found out, that he is not military personnel, and he is not American either.*"

He listened for some time, and wrote a full page in the notebook in front of him, and kept saying "Yes Sir, Yes Sir."

"*I will write the letter to them today, and will send you a copy. I don't know, how this happened in the first place. This is the first time, I have come across such a case, with failures all along the way.*"

The sergeant ordered himself a coffee, and smoked a cigar, before picking up the phone to speak with WHO's medical services coordinator's office in Geneva.

"*Hello. Am I speaking to the Medical Services Co-ordinator?*"

"*Yes, you are. How can I help you?*"

"*This is Sergeant Riley from Ramstein American Airbase Hospital. I am calling you regarding one of your employees, a Sudanese national with the name Dr Omer Mekki, who was mistakenly transferred to our facility, from Iraq, after the Canal Hotel explosion. We have been looking after him, and now his general condition is good, and stable. Although, this was a mistake on our part, our rule stipulates, that only American servicemen are admitted to our military base hospital. Accordingly, I am giving you two hours, to remove your employee from our facility, otherwise, we are going to send him back to Iraq. I must tell you that we have already started our transfer procedure to Iraq. Sorry, we are just following our procedures.*"

"*Thank you very much for looking after him. In fact, Dr Omer was listed as missing, and unaccounted for, and we didn't know his whereabouts. I am very pleased to hear, that he is well, and in good* hands. I am certain, that we will be able to evacuate him from your facility, in the next hour or so. I would be grateful, if you could send me an up-to-date, and detailed medical report, for the purpose of the transfer. The Air Ambulance crew will be co-ordinating with you. Is there anything you want to add?"

"I will send you the medical report by email now. Please do stick to the two hours ultimatum, which starts the minute we finish this conversation".

"Will start my stopwatch now," he said jokingly, and hung up. He couldn't understand, why they were given only two hours to do the transfer, and what was all the urgency for, and the threat to take Dr Omer back to Iraq, where he might die, considering what the Americans had done to the healthcare infrastructure. The guy shook his head in disbelief, and murmured, "Strange Americans. They don't care, do they?"

Luckily, the WHO had only recently signed a contractual agreement with an Air Ambulance company, to carry out emergency evacuation of its employees in any situation. They also had an agreement with a University Hospital in Geneva, to receive any of its employees who needed emergency medical care. Unknown to him, Dr Omer would be the first beneficiary of these agreements.

Joh Doe (now Dr Omer Mekki) noticed, that there was an increased activity around him. He had a bed bath, and changed into a different set of clothes. His vital signs were checked again, and his wounds cleaned, and redressed. He could see the nurses, and doctors going over his medical records, and updating them. No one told him what this was all about. He didn't bother to ask either. He was tired, and just wanted to be left alone. Then the hectic activity came to an end, and the nurse told him, that he was going to be transferred to a hospital in Geneva. He looked at her vacantly and said nothing.

Four people in reflective, orange outfits came into the room, accompanied by his nurse, Private Stone. They quickly examined him, checked his vital signs, and looked into his medical records.

"We are the team, who is going to accompany you to Geneva. Do you understand?" Dr Omer nodded, without opening his eyes.

The nurse told them, that he had no belongings, whatsoever. This information was met by raised eyebrows from the emergency ambulance team.

They professionally transferred, and strapped him to a stretcher, and wheeled him out to a waiting road ambulance. This drove a short distance to an airstrip, inside the air base, where an Air Ambulance was waiting.

During the short flight to Geneva, which took less than two hours, Dr Omer felt unwell in a strange way. Some funny headaches, made him feel slightly sick, and dizzy. He couldn't concentrate and felt he was drifting away, and becoming confused.

He was admitted to the University Hospital in Geneva, and given a full examination, and a battery of investigations. It became clear that he was again having an intra-cranial bleeding, and he needed a third craniotomy, to evacuate the resulting hematoma.

On the following day, after the operation; his condition started to steadily improve. Since the accident, all the medical attention had been directed towards the head injury, as it was the one which could have killed him. Now that this had been almost sorted out, attention was directed to the facial injuries. The right side of his face was a mess, with lacerations of different depths, and with pieces of flesh missing. There were also signs of injury to the facial nerve. This nerve is responsible for the movements of the muscles on its side of the face. When injured, that side of the face is paralysed, and the face becomes asymmetrical. Also, you can't close your eye on the paralysed side. You can't whistle, and you dribble from the corner of your mouth.

There were also injuries on the upper part of his neck, and under his chin. This area is very crowded with important, and vital structures, including major arteries, and veins going to and from the brain, plus the windpipe, and the gullet. Injury to any of these might be fatal. Shrapnel travelling at a very high velocity, can rip structures and cause severe damage, it can even rip limbs off.

One day, while the doctors were gathered around his bed, doing their morning medical round, Dr Omer asked the neurosurgeon,

"Can I, please, have a phone to make a call?"

"Whom are you going to ring?" asked the neurosurgeon with a mixture of disbelief, and worry painted all over his face. Disbelief, because he didn't think Dr Omer would be able to remember any phone number to ring after all he had been through, and worry because he might be talking gibberish due to a brewing intracranial bleeding.

"I would like to make two phone calls, one to my wife, and another to my friend Walid."

"OK. Tell me the number, and I will dial it for you." There was a ringing tone, and then a lady answered the call. He handed the device to Dr Omer.

"Hello Thuraya. How are you? It is Omer." There was an eerie silence for a few seconds. All the members of the medical team were listening in anticipation, the neurosurgeon stood there, with his jaw dropping.

There followed a long conversation in Arabic, with tears welling up in Dr Omer's left eye. He knew now, his wife would be arriving soon, and that the rest of the family was fine.

"Can you please dial this number too?" The neurosurgeon dialled the number, and gave him the phone.

"Salamualaikum, Walid. This is Dr Omer from Geneva."

"Oh, my God! Dr Omer, how are you and nice to hear from you."

"I am fine, but still in hospital, and probably, will stay here for some time. Please tell all our friends, not to worry. I will send you the contact number soon. Sorry I can't talk much." Everyone was flabbergasted. How could he remember those numbers, after all that messing with his brain? Remembering things after such an injury is something, but remembering phone numbers is completely out of this world. No one was expecting that. Dr Omer did not think much of it. He always had a good memory, so what was the big deal?

⚜

Chapter 19

THE REUNION

His wife arrived from Saudi Arabia. He immediately recognized her, said the right words, and asked the appropriate questions. As for her, she just cried, and cried, and cried. Seeing him in bandages and with a twisted face, was not easy to bear. She was afraid to hug him, just in case she broke something, or pushed something out of its place.

"Are you ok?" she asked

"As you can see, am fine," he replied with an internal smile, which he couldn't paint on what was left of his face. She had to get used to him speaking slowly, through the left side of his mouth.

"How did you end up here?"

"I have no idea. The last thing I remember was, that after I spoke to you on the phone, I went into the Canal Hotel to attend the meeting, and sat in a room with a group of people. Then I woke up in a hospital somewhere, and then was transferred here. They told me here, that there was an accident, but I didn't ask about any details."

"At this stage I think you should concentrate on getting better, and you will get better, inshallah. Can you eat normally?"

"Yes, I can with some discomfort and difficulty. Now, am living on warm fluids through a straw. I have soups, milk, juices, and so on. When I go home, you don't need to cook for me," he said that, with the now familiar unseen smile.

"Are your teeth all there?"

Omer didn't answer, so she repeated the question. Omer remained silent, with his left eye closed. Thuraya panicked, and shouted for the nurses.

"What is the matter?" asked the nurse calmly

"He is not talking back to me, and keeping his eye closed. We were chatting normally, only a minute ago," answered Thuraya, with all the worry in the world on her face.

"OK let us see," the nurse checked the monitors, took his blood pressure, and gently shook his left shoulder. Omer opened his eyes, and answered the nurse, that he was fine.

"He is just tired and too weak, to hold a conversation for a long time. No need to worry. Just try to keep your conversation short. He is recovering very well, considering what he has been through. I think you should go, and have some rest too. We will look after him." The nurse, then walked away, with a reassuring, heavenly smile.

Thuraya looked at Omer, and she could see that he was just asleep. He looked peaceful. She said a silent prayer, and left for her room. She flung herself onto the bed, and went to sleep thinking of the reassuring smile on the nurse's face. Woke up suddenly at midnight. At first, she didn't know where she was, but after some recollection, it dawned on her she was in Geneva, thousands of miles from home and the children, with her husband in a hospital bed. This made her depressed, and worried at the same time, and gave her insomnia for the rest of the night. She kept tossing, and turning in bed, but finally sprang out of bed, and made herself a cup of black coffee, and sat on a chair looking out of the window.

The streets outside were quiet, and deserted, apart from the occasional passing car, and the sound of a distant siren of an ambulance or a police car. There was not a single star in the sky. This was in contrast to the Milky way you see, every time you look up at the night sky in Sudan. She looked through some books, but they were all in French.

"Is French the national language of Switzerland? Is There a Swiss language?" she asked herself.

Her body clock was totally confused. She had no idea what the time was, or even, what day it was. Around mid-morning, she stepped out of the bathroom, after a long, hot bath. She felt even more tired. She had some coffee, and biscuits, and a bar of chocolate. The orange juice *didn't taste like the one in Saudi, its nature and freshness had been tampered with.*

Today, Omer was going to be taken to the operating room, to have his facial wounds cleaned, and debrided. They found that the duct leading from his Parotid (salivary) gland was lacerated, and leaking saliva into the wound. They needed to put a stent into the lumen of the duct across the laceration, to divert the flow of saliva into the mouth.

When Thuraya walked into the room, the bed was empty. She checked the bathroom. He was not there. The nurse who came in, spoke only French. She acted normally, wrote something on the medical records hanging at the foot of the bed, made sure that the monitors were working, and then just waited there. Minutes later the door flung open, and Omer was wheeled in.

His bandages seem to have become bigger now, covering most of his face and head. He was still under the after effect of the anaesthetic, but he was continuously moaning, and sounded restless. After connecting Omer to the monitors, the nurse gave Thuraya a reassuring look, decorated with a beaming smile.

Seeing the worried look on Thuraya's face, an English-speaking nurse was brought in, who explained what had been done in the morning. What she said was very reassuring, and music to Thuraya's ears.

Omer's moaning and restlessness settled, and he slept like a baby. She pulled a chair, and sat beside the bed, holding his hand and performing a prayer, asking God for his complete recovery.

After some time, Omer was well enough to be transferred to a rehabilitation centre, as he didn't need a hospital bed anymore. He still needed more plastic and reconstructive procedures to try and give him his face back. For this he could go into the hospital, have the procedure. And come back.

One day, Thuraya slipped on a wet patch on the floor, and fell awkwardly. The housekeeping lady had just finished wiping the floor, but forgot to put the wet floor sign. She felt severe pain in her left leg, and she couldn't get up. Omer rang the emergency services, who arrived after a short time. They helped her onto a stretcher, and rushed her to the Emergency Room. There was an obvious swelling on her shin, and the pain was unbearable. She was given some painkillers, and had an X-Ray of her leg. It was broken, and needed fixing. She was transferred to an Orthopaedic hospital, outside Geneva.

She had come here to support Omer, and look after him, now she needed someone to look after her. How was she going to manage? She cried and cried.

"Unfortunately, your leg is broken. The good news is, that the break is a simple one which makes the operation straight forward," explained the orthopaedic surgeon.

"My husband is an inpatient in a hospital in Geneva, and I am the only next of kin here to look after him. How long, before I become mobile again?"

"You might need about one week, before we are able to discharge you. Normally we discharge patients in 48 hours, but we need to keep you longer, because of your uncontrolled diabetes, and high blood pressure."

For ten days, they were patients in different hospitals. Omer managed to go, and visit her, and found that she was recovering well.

"I don't want to stay in this hospital."

"Why? What happened?"

"People here have no empathy. They tell you, that you have diabetes, and high blood pressure, without even blinking, as if it is a normal thing to have these horrible diseases. They tell you all the possible complications in one big dose."

"This is how they do things here. Remember you are not in Sudan."

"I just don't want to stay here."

Omer asked his friend, the Sudanese ambassador to try, and make her change her mind. The ambassador used all his diplomatic magic, and skills, and she agreed to stay.

Omer was having, yet, another operation. This time it was a skin graft to cover a defect in his right cheek near the angle of the mouth. Omer was resigned to the fact, that he would be in and out of the operating room, for the next few months, having tubes, and wires inserted into his veins or stuck onto his skin, monitors beeping, and flashing all the time, disturbing his sleep, and would be taking pills of different colours, and shapes, and meeting people wearing different uniforms, and speaking a funny language.

Thuraya, now, was walking with the help of crutches which she found very awkward, and nerve racking, despite encouragement, and reassurance from the physiotherapist. She was developing a "walk phobia". She had this nightmare of falling, and breaking her other leg. She thought, that the blood pressure tablets made her dizzy, and she would deliberately miss a dose or two. Her doctor was baffled, as to why her blood pressure control was so erratic.

All in all, Omer stayed in Geneva hospitals for a total of six months; from August 2003 to February 2004. Staying in an institution, that being a hospital or a prison, is boring, and monotonous. It numbs your brain, and makes you feel like a robot. Your brain faces no challenges, and becomes lazy. You tend to live in a bubble of your own, and forget about what is happening outside in the wider world. You become institutionalised. This is a disease condition in itself, with all its mental and psychological aftermath.

It was no surprise, that Omer and his wife spent hours talking on the phone to family, relatives, and friends. They needed to keep abreast with the latest news from Baghdad, and the fate of their friends. The kids were ringing every day, and sometimes, twice a day, and talking for hours giving a full report of what was happening, and not happening. They were missing, and worried about dad, and felt, that talking to him on the phone was the only way for them to be close to him.

One day Mr Behbahani, WHO employee based in Geneva, brought two mobile phones; one for Omer and one for his wife.

"These devices are for your personal use,"

"For our personal use? How come?"

"The hospital management contacted me, complaining that their telephone lines are almost continuously engaged by calls coming to, or made by Dr Omer and his wife. They threatened to move you out if this didn't stop."

"Oh. We are very sorry. I didn't realise that we were causing all that problem."

"I appreciate the situation you are in, and the need to contact your loved ones. From now on you can use these phones."

WHO employee, Khalid Shabeeb, was in Baghdad when the Canal Hotel explosion happened. He was based in Geneva, but was seconded to Baghdad, as a member of the Emergency Services in Crisis team. He knew Omer from previous encounters. His wife, who was in Geneva at the time, visited Omer in the hospital.

"Khalid said to give you this money just in case you need it."

"Money?" Omer exclaimed with a loud laugh. "What will I need money for? I hardly leave this room, and when I do, it is usually on a trolley. My stay here is full board. Where shall I put it, these hospital gowns have no pockets," he said, between the laughs.

"Please keep it. I will put it in the bedside cabinet." Then she left, after wishing him a speedy recovery.

Omer didn't even bother to see how much the money was, but marvelled at the thoughtfulness and kindness of his friend Khalid, and thanked God that he had friends like him. Omer had many good and kind friends, because he himself was always kind and supportive towards others. He never hesitated in giving his time, effort, knowledge, and even his own money, for those who needed it. He was liked and respected by all.

It was a huge surprise, but a very pleasant one, when Khalid Shabeeb walked into the room.

"Alsalmualaikum Dr Omer. How nice to see you looking so well," carefully hugging him.

"Wa Alaikum Alsalam. It is doubly nice to see you, my friend. What are you doing here, and how is everyone back in Baghdad?"

"I just finished my stint in Baghdad, and of course, I couldn't wait to leave. After the Canal Hotel explosion, we are all feeling very unsafe and vulnerable. Security has been beefed up around us, but still, we feel insecure. In Baghdad itself shootings, killings, bombing and explosions are carrying on unabated."

"That is sad, isn't it? Iraq is no more. That great country destroyed for no fault of its own," Omer commented, with a tinge of sadness all over his face, well on the left side of his face.

"Many of our colleagues, who experienced the explosion first hand, found it very difficult to carry on working and have resigned, and left Iraq all together. Some are undergoing intensive psychotherapy and counselling."

"Did you manage to do any useful work lately?"

"We manage to lay down the basics of Emergency Services in Crisis, mainly in Baghdad, although, the crisis is all over Iraq. It is so hard as the Americans have different ideas which suit them only, and their priorities are different. So many challenges and obstacles."

"But we must persevere for the sake of humanity. That is our job and mission."

"I know, but some people can take only that much. I shouldn't bother you with a lot of grim news, and let you rest." Khalid then stood up, took out a bulging small envelope from his pocket, and handed it over to Omer.

"Do you recognize this?" Omer started opening the envelope with eagerness and anticipation.

"Oh. This looks like my wallet, and these are my credit cards. Where the hell did you get this from?" asked Omer, with astonishment on the left side of his face.

"Dr Popal and Walid went to the American field hospital in Albalad to look for you, as you were unaccounted for after the explosion. There, the nurse gave them the wallet, which she found in a pocket of what was left of your trousers. When they heard, that I am coming to Geneva, they asked me to deliver it to you."

"That is amazing. Unbelievable!"

"Also, this is your telephone, which you left in your office in the WHO Headquarters."

"Oh, thanks a million. This is really valuable; it has the names of all my contacts."

Khalid then excused himself, and promised to visit again.

Omer kept looking at the wallet, and wondering how come it was not damaged, and if his trousers had been torn to pieces, how come his legs escaped injury? He quickly dismissed these queries, as he had already decided not to chase any details of what had happened. He believed that knowing no details, at least for the time being, would help preserve his sanity. All he knew was, that he was injured in an explosion, ended up here in Geneva, and he was getting better by the day. That was enough, thank you.

"You know, the money given to me by the WHO has almost run out. How are we going to manage?" Thuraya said with a resigned look on her face.

"Don't worry, something will come up."

"What do you mean, don't worry, aren't you worried; we need money. You need to sort something out."

"I will go and get some cash from downstairs now," Omer said, with a strange half smile peering through the bandages. Thuraya immediately got worried. Cash money from downstairs? What money and how? She thought, something happened to make him talk gibberish.

"Are you ok? Do you want me to call the nurse?"

"Yes."

"Hello. Can I be of any help," said the nurse in rehearsed English.

"I am just asking, if I can go and get some cash from the ATM (Automated Teller Machine) downstairs?" The nurse and Thuraya exchanged perplexed glances, but said nothing.

"Can I?"

"Of course, you can, but you need your bank card, and you need to remember the PIN." She glanced at Thuraya, as if asking for support.

"I know that. Can I go then?"

"From my part you can go, but you have to come on time for your medicine, in about thirty minutes." The nurse went, and looked at his record, and found that all was well. She couldn't find an explanation for his latest behaviour. She would wait and see after he comes back, before entering this episode into his medical record.

Omer and Thuraya went down to the ground floor, where the ATM was located together with a couple of cafes and fast-food outlets. Thuraya eyed him suspiciously, not knowing what to expect.

"Let us have some coffee first," he pulled a chair and sat down.

"I don't have any money on me. Do you?"

"No. I will withdraw some money."

They had their coffee, and chatted for a bit. All that he was saying made sense, and his general behaviour seemed normal. He then got up, and walked towards the ATM. He stood there for a while, Thuraya watching him closely.

"The bill please." He indicated to the waitress, seating himself down. He paid the bill, and tipped the waitress for her good service and nice smile.

"We'd better go back for my medicine." Thuraya's jaw dropped. What the hell?

Omer laughed. He told her the story of the wallet, but couldn't explain, even to himself, how he remembered the PIN, but again he remembered the phone numbers before, which is more difficult than the PIN. Might be, his brain injury didn't affect the small, nerve tissue drawers where he kept his memory or might even have made his memory sharper.

The nurse couldn't believe what she heard. She had always suspected, that human brain is a mysterious and ill-understood thing, now her suspicion was confirmed. How could you remember a PIN, after sustaining a major head injury when you were in a deep coma for five days? When she told the rest of the team, they thought she was joking. Some of them had to keep their bank card PIN in their mobile phone, to refer to as they often forgot it.

Days went by slowly. Monotony was the name of the game. Boredom and helplessness bit deep into their patience. They were hovering on the edge of depression. They missed the kids and the extended family. There was no clear indication, as to when all this was going to end. Ignorance of the French language was a big disadvantage and a limiting factor. The misery of winter was fast approaching. For them it was already cold, having come from 50 degrees Celsius Iraq. The sun's share of the 24-hour day was getting shorter and shorter, and its rays didn't sting anymore, when it got the chance to peer through the clouds. People lose their sense of humour and become withdrawn, in such weather. Rate of depression and suicide goes up steeply.

Omer's movements were curtailed by the fact, that he was in and out of the operating room, having all sorts of plastic surgery done on his head, face, and neck. These operations needed him to come multiple times to the hospital, for the wounds to be inspected, and the dressings changed, and also plans made for further action. Surgeons always advised him to take it easy, and rest, to help wound healing.

Thuraya's movements were curtailed by the fact, that her mobility was very much reduced after her leg fracture. This was compounded by her severe phobia of walking, and her lack of confidence. To venture out, she had to put on many layers of clothes, and even that were not warm enough.

They missed Sudanese cuisine. The exotic ingredients were not available here. Food here had no taste, and was very bland. They were always conscious of not eating any food, which contained pig meat. There was no Halal meat here. They lived on sea food and vegetables. Although this was enough to sustain them, they missed Halal lamb and beef.

They missed family gatherings, chatting, and joking in Arabic. They missed the loud laughs to jokes, which were not as funny, when translated into another language. They missed the home brewed coffee. They missed the heat, the sun, the ceiling fans, the air coolers, the sun umbrellas, and the early afternoon siesta. They missed people of colour, with black hair and black eyes. They missed the real life.

Sometimes they spent the whole day without talking to anyone, apart from those concerned with their treatment and rehabilitation. This was usually official niceties, decorated with what seemed like an AI-generated smile. Genuine smiles from the core of truthfulness were a rarity around here.

They stayed in Geneva from August 2003 till February 2004; whole six months, during which Omer had almost thirteen operative procedures. He won the medal of the longest serving foreign patient, in the surgical department of this University hospital. He made a few friends, and learnt a little bit of French.

At the end of this period, Omer was discharged from hospital care, but had to come for review at a three-month interval, with the possibility of further plastic surgery procedures on his face.

He almost regained his lost face. He was still recognizable to those who knew him. His trademark, the bushy moustache, hadn't changed. He had lost the right Parotid salivary gland, and the right, facial nerve. This nerve controls the movements of the facial muscles, on the right side. The unopposed pull of the facial muscles on the left side tilted the whole face to the left, resulting in a noticeable asymmetry. If you looked closely enough, you could notice, that his right eye didn't close shut, and the right angle of his mouth drooped a little. What you couldn't see were small Titanium plates and screws inserted into his broken, facial bones, and larger plates replacing some of his skull bones. The Titanium man.

Thuraya was walking gingerly, but confidently, and with no noticeable limp. The long Titanium plate and screws used to fix her fracture were still there.

"I think Titanium is an expensive metal, and if I need money, I will remove this hardware and sell it." She used to joke. At the time of writing this book, the hardware is still firmly fixed to her shin bone. I can only assume that at the moment; she is doing fine from the financial point of view, but saving the Titanium for a rainy day.

Dr Omer was still on the WHO payroll, during his long hospital stay and recuperation. Before his final discharge from the hospital, he underwent a thorough physical, neurological, psychological, and behavioural assessment. The conclusion was, that he suffered no sequelae from his injuries, and he was fit as a fiddle. On the basis of this, the WHO was happy for him to go back to work.

From Geneva, he went and started working in the Amman office in Jordan. There he noticed, that people were trying to be nicer to him, and not to bother him, and even do some of his work for him. He immediately stamped out this behaviour, and proved to them, that he was his old self.

Days went by slowly and monotonously. Subjects of discussion were mostly about the Canal Hotel explosion, and those who lost their lives, and the security risk which was still hanging over the WHO and the United Nations employees. Many employees were now reluctant to go to Iraq, despite the assurance that security had been beefed up.

Dr Omer continued to work in Amman, and do short missions in Baghdad. The Green Area was established by the Americans, where they built their heavily fortified embassy. This green area also housed governmental ministries and the offices of the United Nations and World Health Organization. It was the safest area in Baghdad, although, attacks and explosions continued to occur inside it. In 2011, Dr Omer applied for retirement. He was requested to stay another year, as they needed his valuable expertise and knowledge, and for them to recruit a suitable replacement.

In 2012, Dr Omer officially retired from the WHO. Soon after that, and before he took the first steps on the road of retirement, the Centre for Disease Control (CDC) approached him to come and work for them. They knew about the good work he had done in Iraq and Saudi Arabia, and that he would be a valuable asset for them.

The only problem was, that they wanted him to go and work in Iraq. For them, he was the most suitable candidate as he had worked in Iraq, and most importantly, he had done a very good job there. But, would he agree to be based in Iraq, after what happened?

"First, I must say how happy I am to see you looking so well, after that horrific explosion."

"Thank you very much, but, if you don't mind, I don't really want to be reminded of that incident. It seems, whenever people meet me all they want is to talk about it." The CDC guy sank in his chair. If Dr Omer didn't even want to talk about the accident, what chance was there, that he was going to accept going to Iraq again?

"I am very sorry," he said apologetically. "We would like you to work for us. This is not an interview in the real sense of the word, because we know who you are and your portfolio. This is a job offer."

"I hardly enjoyed any retirement. I have many friends in CDC, and we worked together on many projects. Let me have a look at the contract. I think, I still have a lot to offer."

"I would like to let you know, that this job will be based in Baghdad. You will reside and work from the Green Area. You will move out of the Green Area in military convoys. The only snag is that you will not be able to bring your family."

"I am aware of these arrangements. While working in Amman, I used to do short stints in Baghdad. The Green Area is secure, but too much security sometimes gives you a sense of insecurity and imminent danger, if you know what I mean."

"Yes. I know what you mean."

Going out of the Green Area to work, Dr Omer would insert himself in this Humvee armoured car, which was part of a long convoy of funny looking army vehicles. The convoy was led by a combined force of Iraqi and American army.

In one of these outings, the convoy passed in front of the Canal Hotel. Dr Omer took a quick glance at it, and then looked away. A shiver went down his spine, and a strange feeling overwhelmed him. Something deep down wanted him to have another look at the hotel, but, even a stronger something forced him to tell the driver to put his foot down, and get him out of this neighbourhood as fast as possible. This place had become a part of him and his life history. Mention Dr Omer, the Canal Hotel popped up; mention the Canal Hotel and Dr Omer's name popped up.

The Canal Hotel itself, had been demolished, in part or in toto, and rebuilt. Dr Omer was not interested in the least, in what had become of it.

Some might find it strange, and I don't blame them, that Dr Omer chose to go back, and work in Iraq again. You would expect that Dr Omer would never go anywhere near that country, which almost cost him his life. I was also surprised that he went back to Iraq, so I asked him why.

"Normally, I am frightened of death. But who isn't? I used to get in a state, when I fall ill because of the thought of death. I used to run to the hospital, and do a lot of tests, for the slightest of symptoms. People used to laugh at me when I don my mask, if anyone sneezes near me. I religiously wash my hands, for fear of catching a bug. I double check every step I take."

"This sounds to me more like an obsessive compulsive personality," I interjected.

"Could be, but this has been ruled out by a psychiatrist friend," he said laughingly.

"Now, after the incident, I found out that I don't care. Even when I am crossing the street, I don't look properly. Isn't that crazy? I don't fear death anymore, and I don't even think about it. When I was asked to work in Iraq, the danger and the risk side of the equation didn't come into play in my decision making."

"That is very strange. Could it be, that fear has a special centre in the brain, which in your case has been put out of action by the accident?" I said speculatively.

"I haven't heard about your new theory before. You need to do some more research to prove it."

"Sure, I will do that, and I will use you as my study case".

"The scans won't be able to spy on my head, because it is armour-plated now." Omer said, gently tapping the side of his head making a funny metallic sound.

"Has anything else changed in you after the incident?"

"I was hoping you or somebody will tell me. I haven't noticed anything myself."

"Didn't your wife or kids say anything to you?"

"No, but I feel that they are very nice to me."

"Were they not nice to you before."

"Now they are nicer," he said, with a wink.

"I tell you what, life now is more beautiful and more enjoyable. The grass is a lot greener, birds chirping at dawn is more amazing, *the written word carries more meaning than ever, the spoken word is more truthful than ever, and human beings are more human than ever."*

"I have noticed a definite change in you," I said with an air of confidence.

"And what is that, Mr Know it all?"

"You have become a philosopher; this is definitely a positive change."

"What is positive about being a philosopher?"

"Philosophers tell us what is the real meaning of life, the hidden cryptic meanings, which we don't normally think about. They always look at life from a different angle and through a different lens. I am sure you have read or heard about the great Greek philosophers, like Aristotle and Socrates, and the famous Chinese philosopher Confucius, and more recently John Rawls, who was arguably the most important, political philosopher of the twentieth century, and many others."

"The problem is that nobody understands what they say, although, some people pretend they do."

"You are a philosopher now. You can tell me. what it is all about." I leant forward, expecting Omer to say something important, but he just looked at me, and started checking his phone. It seems philosophy didn't come into his field of interest. I got the message. Most probably, he thought I was taking the mickey.

I was.

I think I am allowed to take the mickey out of my friends, or so the saying goes.

"Shall we change this subject of philosophy, because I am not a philosopher, and I don't understand anything about philosophy. I will not be able to engage in any meaningful conversation." With this the matter was closed.

The two years in Iraq (2012- 2014) went slowly, but smoothly. Anxiety and uncertainty were the new normal. Anxiety about "are you going to come back home alive or are you going to be the next victim?"

Road-side bombs, explosions, random shootings, kidnappings, and disappearances were daily occurrences.

Uncertainty as to whether the daily task was going to be done, or going to be cancelled at the last minute, because of a security concern. Uncertainty, that the staff who lived outside the Green Area would attend or had they been killed the night before.

Despite the huge challenges, and the unusual circumstances, under which they had been working, Dr Omer and team had done a great job in pushing back the frontiers of Polio and other childhood diseases. They spent the whole day doing field work. In the evening, after a short rest, they wrote reports and discussed the next day's plans, before going to bed for a well-deserved rest and sleep. They found respite in the R and R (Rest and Recuperation). This was a two-week break every six months, which they usually spent in Amman, where they switched off and enjoyed life. These two weeks usually felt like a few days, and they soon found themselves back in the grinding and relentless machine of life in Iraq, and in the large prison called the Green Area.

The two years in Iraq came to an end, and Dr Omer was to go as a contractor to Somalia, another hot spot. He welcomed the transfer without hesitation, paying no attention to the dangers ahead. This was now normal for him. He didn't fear death anymore. The "fear centre" in his brain had been made redundant by the accident. He thought this was a good thing. Why bother if your fate has already been decided? People believe that everyone is going to die at a certain time and in a certain place, and whatever you do you can't change that. This might explain the miraculous escape from a horrible accident, or being in the wrong place at the wrong time. The other and more reasonable side of the argument is, not to put yourself in danger, and always take reasonable precautions to protect yourself. Arguments rage when people discuss this issue, but usually end without agreement.

Although Dr Omer was happy to go to Somalia and face a new challenge, his happiness was tinged with some sadness. The sadness of saying farewell to his friends, whom he knew and worked with, and especially those, who had helped him at the time of his great need. He would miss the Iraqi families and their joy, when they were told that their children are now protected against Polio and other childhood diseases. Some of these families had older children, who were affected by Polio and knew what that meant.

He would not miss sitting in that car, going in a military convoy to work. He would definitely not miss the American soldiers, the sound of gunfire, the explosions, the continuous buzzing of military helicopters flying overhead, and that horrible screeching sound of the heavy iron gate at the entrance to the Green Area. Dr Omer wondered, how those guards could stand that annoying noise day in and day out. Why couldn't someone oil those bloody hinges?

Most of the work for Somalia was done from the Kenyan capital, Nairobi. I myself visited Nairobi in 1974 while I was in the final year medical school, and stayed for one week. It was a lovely city with clean tree-lined streets. Most of its buildings are not more than five stories high, and the skyline is dominated by the multistorey Hilton Hotel. There were nice pubs and night spots, and the city centre has elegant shops, including some of the famous brand names. Nairobi used to be called little London.

Now Dr Omer is telling me that Nairobi has grown enormously, both vertically and horizontally. More multi-storey buildings have sprung up all over the central part of the city, while shanty towns were on the periphery. This distribution reflects the haves and have-nots. It is more crowded now, and traffic jams are a part of daily life.

Dr Omer was conducting the work in Somalia by remote control from Nairobi. Somalia at that time was unstable and unsafe. Another colleague went to Mogadishu to do the field work, and report back to the main office in Nairobi. This was the standing arrangement, and had nothing to do with the security situation in Somalia. It might be, the staff there thought Dr Omer had his fair share of horror and trauma, and deserved a break. Dr Omer himself had no qualms of going to Mogadishu.

Dr Omer visited Somaliland many times and did some field work there. Somaliland (officially the Republic of Somaliland) is an unrecognized country in the horn of Africa. It is located in the southern coast of the Gulf of Aden. It declared its independence from Somalia in 1991, but still, remained an unrecognized country. Despite the lack of international legitimacy, the coastal territory has a relatively stable democracy, and is attracting major foreign investors, but it remains a poor country.

Dr Omer stayed in Nairobi for one year (2014-2015), which he thoroughly enjoyed. Work was very organized, the staff were all very nice, weather was good, and above all, Nairobi is a safe city. He met a lot of Sudanese, who made Kenya their second home. It is always nice to meet your countrymen abroad. Sudanese are known to be very social and nice people, and support and help each other. If you live in a Sudanese community abroad, you don't need to worry about anything; but of course, you have to do your bit too.

At the end of his tenure in Somalia, Dr Omer was on the move again. This time the plane took him east to Pakistan. In Pakistan, he worked in the Northern part of Sindh Province. This is a poor area of Pakistan. Poverty and endemic diseases go hand in hand. The job in hand was to control and eradicate Polio and other childhood diseases. With his vast experience and knowledge, this task was a piece of cake for him.

North Sindh province is the third largest in Pakistan, with an area of almost 148000 square kilometres and a population of around 48 million. It is situated in the southeast of the country, and Karachi is its provincial capital.

Dr Omer stayed in Pakistan till 2022. By the time he left, there were 22 cases of Polio. These came down to six cases in 2023, but went up to seventy-three in 2024 following a Polio outbreak. Pakistan, together with Afghanistan, are considered endemic for Polio.

Dr Omer had to retire in 2022, and go to Sudan. His wife, Thuraya, had an accident and broke her shoulder, and she had to have an urgent operation. Unfortunately, something went wrong with the operation, and things got complicated. Another procedure was performed, but to no avail. Shoulder movements were restricted and painful.

Dr Omer and Thuraya travelled to London in January 2023, to see if something could be done there to render her shoulder functional again. *They didn't choose the right time of the year to come to London, especially when coming from Sudan, where the coldest temperature is in the early twenties. They arrived in the dead of winter; short dark days and long darker nights, freezing rain.*

It was here in London, where I met Dr Omer and Thuraya. I visited them many times in their flat in Paddington area. We chatted like old classmates, recalling the memories of the good old days in the medical school, asking about colleagues and what had become of them, and remembering our professors and mentors, and what a good job they had done to put us on the right path of medical practice.

I must admit that I heard about the Canal Hotel explosion and Dr Omer's injury pretty late.

"How come I didn't hear about this accident? No body told me, and I think most of the colleagues didn't know either."

"I think the main reason is, that we lost contact with most of the colleagues. Some I haven't seen since graduation, just imagine." He said with a shake of the head.

"I do agree. It is a shame. We all were a close-knit group, and one would expect that we would remain a close-knit group. May be, we should track down all the colleagues, and establish a network or something."

"I agree. It will be a difficult task but it is worthwhile."

"I am going to contact all the colleagues I am still in touch with, and ask them to do the same. You also do that. This way we might be able to track down all of them."

"Yes. Let us do that."

"So, tell me about this explosion thing",

"It is a long story."

He started telling me what happened. I was taken aback by his intact memory. He was mentioning minute details of incidents and meetings, with times, dates, and names. Half an hour into his story, I had to excuse myself, as I had a prior engagement, but with the promise to come back, and listen to the rest of the story.

I did come on two more occasions, and listened to the full story. It was fascinating, intriguing, and almost unbelievable.

I did a little bit of research about the Canal Hotel explosion. I went through what was written in the media about the incident at the time. I read statements made by WHO officials, interviews conducted with survivors, and family, and friends of the deceased. To my astonishment, and to the best of my knowledge, there was no mention of Dr Omer. That was when I decided to tell his story, and he reluctantly agreed.

Dr Omer left London late in 2023, and because of the deteriorating conditions in Sudan he elected to go to Kenya. Now he is living in a leafy suburb of Nairobi with his wife Thuraya and his two daughters.

In October 2024, we went together for a four-day safari in the Massai Mara, and that was something out of this world.

⊷⊶◅❯⊷⊶

www.ingramcontent.com/pod-product-compliance
Ingram Content Group UK Ltd.
Pitfield, Milton Keynes, MK11 3LW, UK
UKHW020051131025
463845UK00012B/3

9 781835 387689